The World's Best Poetry

Supplement V

Twentieth Century Women Poets

Poetry Anthology Press

The World's Best Poetry

Survey of American Poetry

The World's Best Poetry

Supplement V

Twentieth Century Women Poets

Prepared by
The Editorial Board, Roth Publishing, Inc.

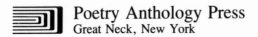 Poetry Anthology Press
Great Neck, New York

The acknowledgements on pages 349–356
constitute a continuation of this copyright
notice.

Library of Congress Catalog Number 82-84763
International Standard Book Number 0-89609-270-4

Manufactured in the U.S.A.

Poetry Anthology Press is a
division of Roth Publishing, Inc.

CONTENTS

PREFACE

The publications of **Poetry Anthology Press** constitute a comprehensive conspectus of international verse in English designed to form the core of a library's poetry collection. Covering the entire range of poetic literature, these anthologies encompass all topics and national literatures.

Each collection, published in a multivolume continuing series format, is devoted to a major area of the whole undertaking and contains complete author, title, and first line indexes. Biographical data is also provided.

The World's Best Poetry, with coverage through the 19th century, is topically classified and arranged by subject matter. Supplements keep the 10 volume foundation collection current and complete.

Survey of American Poetry is an anthology of American verse arranged chronologically in 10 volumes. Each volume presents a significant period of American poetic history, from 1607 to 1984. *Annual Survey of American Poetry* continues the coverage and maintains the currency of the collection.

INTRODUCTION

The first documented poet was a woman from ancient Sumeria named Enheduanna (ca. 2300 B.C.). Though women have continuously written poetry throughout the following centuries, the work of only a small number of poets, such as Otomo No Sakanoe, Sappho, Li Ch'ing Chao, Marie de France, Christine de Pisan, Elizabeth Barrett Browning and Emily Dickinson, has been preserved and has come to represent the familiar canon of poetry by women, from antiquity to the nineteenth century. Even now, in the late twentieth century, when excellent poetry by women is flourishing, most gender-neutral anthologies are edited by males and the selection of male poets routinely predominates. By and large, poetry by men has established the norm in matters of style and subject matter and has inscribed on the popular imagination images of the world and women's place in it, images which many women have found constricting or inaccurate. By focusing on international women poets, this anthology assembles the diverse styles and voices of many of the most respected contemporary poets writing in or translated into English and provides a forum for women to speak about their own experiences.

The blossoming of women's poetry during the present century is a natural accompaniment to a changing world in which women participate in activities traditionally defined as male and actively engage in self-discovery, self-expression, and the attainment of equal rights. During the last hundred years, there have been two important movements in women's fight for political and social change: the suffragette movement and the feminist movement. The former occurred in various locations around the world during the first half of this century. The latter occurred globally as well, primarily during the second half of this century, focusing on a variety of issues which include birth control, abortion, day care, pornography, domestic violence, rape, lesbian rights, affirmative action, and equal pay.

For many, attaining equal rights under the law, maintaining control over one's body, and preventing violence against women is more than just a political agenda—it is a deeply personal matter. In addition to becoming politically involved, poets such as Adrienne Rich and Marge Piercy give artistic expression to their feelings of rage and inadequacy caused by discrimination, as well as to their sense of freedom and pride in the discovery of new potentials. Other poets such as Louise Bogan and Sylvia Plath turn inward to explore their feelings within the more private sphere of their family or their psyche. However, this introspection is also a form of activism as it helps to establish a broader identity for women. As Nikki Giovanni writes in "Revolutionary Dreams": "if i dreamed natural/ dreams of being a natural/ woman doing what a woman/ does when she's natural/ i would have a revolution."

Feminism is not the only political concern that inspires women to write. Nelly Sachs, the 1966 Nobel Prize winner, survived the Nazi holocaust and wrote poems that memorialize the millions of Jews murdered during the Second World War. Anna Akhmatova, one of the greatest modern Russian poets, was officially silenced in her own country by the Stalin regime but continued to write poetry condemning the horrors of war and the police state. Mozambiquan writer Noémia de Sousa used actions and words to fight the government of Portugal for the freedom of her colonized nation. Ingrid Jonker, the daughter of a prominent South African politician, wrote poems that brim with compassion as she publicly feuded with her father over his party's denial of rights to South African blacks. More recently, Carolyn Forché, an American who spent many months as a reporter in El Salvador, has written poetry that bears witness to the abuse of human rights taking place there.

Women poets have also contributed to the intellectual and literary movements of the last century, especially regarding modernist innovations in style and the role of art in society. Chinese poet Ping

Hsin is one of the creators of hsiao-shih, a compact poetic form influenced by the Japanese haiku. American expatriate Gertrude Stein was an influential force in literature and a friend to the many avant-garde artists in Paris before, during, and after World War I. During this time, Edith Sitwell was at the forefront of England's own avant-garde movement. H.D.'s early work captured the spirit of the imagist movement, while at the same time Anna Akhmatova was writing some of the best acmeist poetry in Russia.

The poems in this anthology are as unique as the individual poets. Even the biological and social experiences that women share do not always lead to the recurrent themes of relationships, childbirth, and childrearing one might expect. Generalizations regarding the poetry become still more difficult to make where concerns are political, philosophical, or psychological. Gender seems to be less of a constriction on the breadth of the poetry than on the experience of being a poet. While there are women who have achieved reputations as major poets of their age, they are the exception in a male-dominated field. It is perhaps the deep commitment to writing, in spite of the obstacles, that unites these poets beyond all that they may or may not share.

Bella Akhmadulina

Bella Akhmadulina, born in 1937 in Moscow, is of Tartar and Italian descent. She attended, and was expelled from, the Gorki Institute of Literature. She has been married several times; her first husband was the well-known Russian poet Yevgeny Yevtushenko.

Akhmadulina has been called one of the most brilliant poets in Russia today. Her first book of poems, *String* (1962), was influenced by the work of Anna Akhmatova; it was criticized by the Soviet government as "superfluous and too intimate." She was not allowed to join the Writers' Union as a poet; however, she did join as a translator.

A book of her poems has appeared in English, *Fever and Other Poems* (1969). Many of the poems in this volume are from her later period, when she had been influenced by Maria Tsvetayeva. These poems are longer and more complex than her earlier work. In the poem "I Swear," dedicated to Tsvetayeva, the word "yelabuga" refers to the name of the town in which the older poet committed suicide and is probably derived from the Tartar word for "devil."

The Waitress

But now a queen is walking by,
her earring slowly swaying.
Humbly each young man lowers his eye
and hears what her foot is saying.

She is rustling with the slide of silk.
Her eyes have moist places.
Suddenly everyone is struck
by the shock of her eyelashes.

How splendidly she walks away!
A waitress, never spilling
an arm-high glass, in the café
under the pale blue ceiling.

The customer reading the menu begins
what she can always expand,
and the snowy lances of the napkins
soar up under her hand.

And the unapproachably severe
starched crown upon her curls
floats over her correct coiffure
as white and cool as pearls.

(Geoffrey Dutton and
Igor Mezhakoff-Koriakin, trs.)

I Swear

To the memory of Marina Tsvetayeva

I swear—
—By that summer photo:
on somebody else's porch,
standing by itself, crooked
as a gallows,
neither leading into the house
nor out of it—
locked
in an all-over armor of furious satin,
high collar hindering the throat's great muscle,
that's how you're sitting—done with song and action,
all the horselike labor of hunger and hustle.

—By that photo:
where you are a child with an astonished smile,
and by the thin angles of your elbows,
irresistibly attracting other children, a child
drawing their faces out of the shadows.

—By the dragging pain of remembering your causes,
when, gulping down the vacuum of grief,
and caught in the choking anger of your broken verses
I clear my throat by coughing till it bleeds.

—By your presence: like a shoplifter I bundled you
into my handbag—to steal you for myself,
forgetting that you are somebody else's—you are taboo,
you belong to God, God wants you for himself.

—By all that your drawn flesh had to withstand
from the hunger that gnawed at your coarse orphaned youth,
and by the blessed, holy motherland
which made an end of you with its rat's tooth.

—By that extraordinary African,
all goodness, you loved as an omen of the bad,
the Negro who was happy watching children,
and by the children themselves, and the Tverskoy Boulevard.

—By your sad resting place in paradise
where you have neither trade nor torment
I swear
to kill
your yelabuga.

—By your yelabuga
so that grandchildren will fall asleep
and the old women will frighten them at night,
not knowing the yelabuga is no more:
—Sleep, my boy or girl! Hush! Keep quiet!
Else the blind yelabuga will come in the door.

Oh, when with all her legs tangling around
she begins to quicken her crawl—then immediately
I'll stamp my steel-tipped heel right down
on her tentacles, and swivel silently.
And then with all my weight on that one heel
I'll jam it in the back of her head and keep quite still.
The green juice of her cubs will scorch
my soles with the caustic of its venom.
The ripe egg from her tail I'll throw
to the depths of earth because they're bottomless,
not saying a word about the porch
and Marina's deathly homelessness.
And I swear by that.
While in the darkness
the yelabuga measures me with her red eye
and swears by the stench of hell
by the toads from the well
that I shall die.

(Geoffrey Dutton and
Igor Mezhakoff-Koriakin, trs.)

Anna Akhmatova

Anna Akhmatova was the pseudonym of Anna Adreyevna Gorenko, perhaps the greatest Russian woman poet. Born in 1888 near Odessa to a retired naval engineer, Akhmatova began writing poetry at the age of eleven. She started to study law in 1907 at Kiev College for Women but lost interest and returned to St. Petersburg (later Leningrad), where she spent most of her life.

As a young woman, Akhmatova became one of the most prominent members of the acmeists, a group of poets reacting against the mystical and esoteric vagueness of the symbolist style then current in Russian poetry. The acmeists strove for clarity, compactness, simplicity, and a fidelity to the appearance and texture of things, as opposed to an evocation of inner truth through the use of symbols and metaphors. In 1910 Akhmatova married Nikolai Gumilev, another leading acmeist, but their marriage was dissolved in 1918. She remarried twice in later life.

Two books of poetry published before the Russian Revolution, *Evening* (1912) and *Rosary* (1914), quickly established her fame as a poet. These early poems focused on the theme of frustrated, unhappy love, always a common subject for Akhmatova. In the collections published just after the revolution—*The White Flock* (1917), *Plantain* (1921), *Anno Domini* (1921)—her range of subjects widened and her control as a poet increased. However, she was soon faced with the official disapproval of the new Soviet government. They denounced her work for its alleged preoccupation with love and God, two "bourgeois and aristocratic" subjects. Her Soviet loyalty became still more suspect when her former husband, Gumilev, was executed in 1923 on charges of anti-Soviet conspiracy. From that year until 1940, Akhmatova's poetry was not published in the Soviet Union.

During the Second World War, Akhmatova remained in Leningrad until the city was blockaded by the German army; she returned in 1944. She was allowed to publish some poems and to hold public readings for a time, but in 1946 her poetry was condemned for "eroticism, mysticism, and political indifference," and she was expelled from the Soviet Writers' Union. Akhmatova's son was arrested three times and spent many years in prison camps between 1932 and 1956; her suffering over this is the basis for her long poem cycle, *Requiem*. After the death of Joseph Stalin, Akhmatova was gradually reaccepted into the Soviet literati. Nevertheless, her long work, *Poem Without a Hero*, was not published in the Soviet Union until 1976, ten years after her death. Akhmatova's poetry is widely translated and is admired around the world for its intensely personal, lyrical quality and controlled imagery.

Reading Hamlet

A barren patch to the right of the cemetery,
behind it a river flashing blue.
You said: "All right then, get thee to a nunnery,
or go get married to a fool..."

It was the sort of thing that princes always say,
but these are words that one remembers.
May they flow a hundred centuries in a row
like an ermine mantle from his shoulders.

(Stanley Kunitz, tr.)

Why Is This Age Worse...?

Why is this age worse than earlier ages?
In a stupor of grief and dread
have we not fingered the foulest wounds
and left them unhealed by our hands?

In the west the falling light still glows,
and the clustered housetops glitter in the sun,
but here Death is already chalking the doors with crosses,
and calling the ravens, and the ravens are flying in.

(Stanley Kunitz, tr.)

Lot's Wife

And the just man trailed God's shining agent,
over a black mountain, in his giant track,
while a restless voice kept harrying his woman:
"It's not too late, you can still look back

at the red towers of your native Sodom,
the square where once you sang, the spinning-shed,
at the empty windows set in the tall house
where sons and daughters blessed your marriage-bed."

A single glance: a sudden dart of pain
stitching her eyes before she made a sound...
Her body flaked into transparent salt,
and her swift legs rooted to the ground.

Who will grieve for this woman? Does she not seem
too insignificant for our concern?
Yet in my heart I never will deny her,
who suffered death because she chose to turn.

(Stanley Kunitz, tr.)

The Last Toast

I drink to our ruined house,
to the dolor of my life,
to our loneliness together;
and to you I raise my glass,
to lying lips that have betrayed us,
to dead-cold, pitiless eyes,
and to the hard realities:
that the world is brutal and coarse,
that God in fact has not saved us.

(Stanley Kunitz, tr.)

Willow

I was raised in checkered silence
in the cool nursery of the young century.
Human voices did not touch me,
it was the wind whose words I heard.
I favored burdocks and nettles,
but dearest to me was the silver willow,
my long companion through the years,
whose weeping branches
fanned my insomnia with dreams.
Oddly, I have survived it:
out there a stump remains. Now other willows
with alien voices intone
under our skies.
And I am silent...as though a brother had died.

(Stanley Kunitz, tr.)

Courage

We know what trembles on the scales,
and what we must steel ourselves to face.
The bravest hour strikes on our clocks:
may courage not abandon us!
Let bullets kill us—we are not afraid,
nor are we bitter, though our housetops fall.
We will preserve you, Russian speech,
from servitude in foreign chains,
keep you alive, great Russian word,
fit for the songs of our children's children,

pure on their tongues, and free.

(Stanley Kunitz, tr.)

This Cruel Age Has Deflected Me...

This cruel age has deflected me,
like a river from its course.
Strayed from its familiar shores,
my changeling life has flowed
into a sister channel.
How many spectacles I've missed:
the curtain rising without me,
and falling too. How many friends
I never had the chance to meet.
Here in the only city I can claim,
where I could sleepwalk and not lose my way,
how many foreign skylines I can dream,
not to be witnessed through my tears.
And how many verses I have failed to write!
Their secret chorus stalks me
close behind. One day, perhaps,
they'll strangle me.
I know beginnings, I know endings too,
and life-in-death, and something else
I'd rather not recall just now.
And a certain woman
has usurped my place
and bears my rightful name,
leaving a nickname for my use,
with which I've done the best I could.
The grave I go to will not be my own.

But if I could step outside myself
and contemplate the person that I am,
I should know at last what envy is.

(Stanley Kunitz, tr.)

The Death of Sophocles

That night an eagle swooped down from the skies onto
   Sophocles' house.
And the garden suddenly rocked with a cry of cicadas.
Already the genius strode toward his immortality,
skirting the enemy camp at the walls of his native city.
Then it was that the king had a strange dream:
Great Dionysus ordered him to lift the siege,
so as not to dishonor the service for the dead
and to grant the Athenians the solace of his fame.

(Stanley Kunitz, tr.)

Claribel Alegría

Though Claribel Alegría was born in 1924 in Estelí, Nicaragua, she grew up in El Salvador and is considered one of the leading poets of that country. She immigrated to the United States in 1943 and eventually received a B.A. from George Washington University. In 1947 she married Darwin J. Flakoll; they live in Deya, Mallorca.

Alegría's works include *Vigils* (1953), *Guest of My Time* (1961), and *Long Distance Call* (1966-69). In 1978 she received the Casa de las Americas Prize in Havana, Cuba. Alegría's poetry is angry and political, but its controlled artistry makes it extremely powerful. *Flowers of the Volcano*, a book of her poems translated into English by Carolyn Forché, appeared in 1982.

We Were Three
To Paco and Rodolfo

It was winter,
there was snow,
it was night,
this is a green day
of doves and sun
of ashes and cries.
The wind pushes me
across the bridge
over the cracked earth
through a dry streambed
strewn with cans.

Death comes to life
here in Deya,
the *torrente*
the stone bridge.
My dead wait
at every corner,
the innocent grillwork of balconies
the filmed mirror of my dead.
They smile from the distance
and wave to me,
they leave the cemetery,
a wall of the dead.
My flesh emits light
and they come to my door
waving their arms.
The bridge was stone,
it was night,
our arms circled each other,
we swayed to our songs,
our breath rose from our mouths
in small, crystalline clouds,
it was winter,
there was snow,
we were three.
Today the earth is dry
and resounds like a drum,
my arms fall to my sides,
I am alone.
My dead stand watch
and send signals to me,
they assail me
in the radio and paper.
The wall of my dead
rises and reaches from Aconcagua to Izalco.
The bridge was stone,
it was night,
no one can say

how they died.
Their persecuted voices are one voice
dying by torture in prison.
My dead arise, they rage.
The streets are empty
but my dead wink at me.
I am a cemetery,
I have no country
and they are too many to bury.

(Carolyn Forché, tr.)

Letter to Time

Dear Sir:
I write this letter on my birthday.
I received your gift. I don't like it.
It is always the same.
As a girl I waited impatient.
I dressed up and went to the street
to talk about it.
Don't be stubborn.
I can still see you playing
chess with my grandfather.
At first your visits were rare.
Soon they became daily
and grandfather's voice
lost its luster.
And you insisted
without respect for his humility,
his gentle soul, his shoes.
Later you courted me.

I was still young
and you with your unchanging face.
A friend of my father's
with one eye on me.
Poor grandfather.
You waited at his death bed for the end.
The walls paled
and there was something else.
An unknown air
floated among the things in the room.
You called to him
and he closed my grandfather's eyes
and looked at me.
I forbid you to come back.
Each time I see you my spine stiffens.
Stop following me.
I beg you.
It has been years since I loved another
and your gifts are no longer of interest.
Why do you wait for me in shop windows,
in sleep's mouth,
beneath the uncertain Sunday sky?
Your greeting tastes of musty rooms.
I saw you the other day with the children.
I knew your suit, the same tweed
when you were my father's friend
and I was a student.
Your ridiculous autumn suit.
Do not come back.
I insist.
Do not linger in my garden.
The children will frighten
and the leaves drop.
I have seen them.
What is the use of all of this?
You will laugh a while
and with that unending laugh

you will still turn up.
The children,
my face,
leaves,
all nothing in your eyes.
You will win.
I knew it when I began.

(Carolyn Forché, tr.)

Margaret Atwood

Margaret Atwood was born in 1939 in Ontario, Canada. As a child, she and her family would go on excursions into the bush country of northern Ontario and Quebec where her father, an entomologist specializing in forest insects, conducted his research. Atwood's first book of poetry, *Double Persephone*, was published in 1961, the year she graduated from Victoria College, University of Toronto. She received an M.A. from Radcliffe College in 1962 and briefly studied Victorian Gothic fantasy at Harvard College. She has taught English literature at universities throughout Canada and has traveled extensively in the United States and Europe. She lives in Toronto with novelist Graeme Gibson and their daughter Jess.

One of Canada's most popular and influential writers, Margaret Atwood's reputation as a poet, novelist, and essayist is international. Her many volumes of poetry include *The Circle Game* (1966), *The Animals in That Country* (1968), *The Journals of Susanna Moodie* (1970), *Power Politics* (1973), *Selected Poems* (1976), *Two-Headed Poems* (1978), and *Interlunar* (1984). She has authored six widely-read novels, including *The Edible Woman* (1969), *Surfacing* (1972), *Lady Oracle* (1976), and *The Handmaid's Tale* (1985), two collections of short stories, and a guide to Canadian literature entitled *Survival* (1972). Atwood is also well-known for her continued support of Canadian culture. In 1982 she edited *The New Oxford Book of Canadian Verse in English*.

The City Planners

Cruising these residential Sunday
streets in dry August sunlight:
what offends us is
the sanities:
the houses in pedantic rows, the planted
sanitary trees, assert
levelness of surface like a rebuke
to the dent in our car door.
No shouting here, or
shatter of glass; nothing more abrupt
than the rational whine of a power mower
cutting a straight swath in the discouraged grass.

But though the driveways neatly
sidestep hysteria
by being even, the roofs all display
the same slant of avoidance to the hot sky,
certain things:
the smell of spilled oil a faint

sickness lingering in the garages,
a splash of paint on brick surprising as a bruise,
a plastic hose poised in a vicious
coil; even the too-fixed stare of the wide windows

give momentary access to
the landscape behind or under
the future cracks in the plaster

when the houses, capsized, will slide
obliquely into the clay seas, gradual as glaciers
that right now nobody notices.

That is where the City Planners
with the insane faces of political conspirators
are scattered over unsurveyed
territories, concealed from each other,
each in his own private blizzard;

guessing directions, they sketch
transitory lines rigid as wooden borders
on a wall in the white vanishing air

tracing the panic of suburb
order in a bland madness of snows.

They Eat Out

In restaurants we argue
over which of us will pay for your funeral

though the real question is
whether or not I will make you immortal.

At the moment only I
can do it and so

I raise the magic fork
over the plate of beef fried rice

and plunge it into your heart.
There is a faint pop, a sizzle

and through your own split head
you rise up glowing;

the ceiling opens
a voice sings Love Is A Many

Splendoured Thing
you hang suspended above the city

in blue tights and a red cape,
your eyes flashing in unison.

The other diners regard you
some with awe, some only with boredom:

they cannot decide if you are a new weapon
or only a new advertisement.

As for me, I continue eating;
I liked you better the way you were,
but you were always ambitious.

Owl Song

I am the heart of a murdered woman
who took the wrong way home
who was strangled in a vacant lot and not buried
who was shot with care beneath a tree
who was mutilated by a crisp knife.
There are many of us.

I grew feathers and tore my way out of her;
I am shaped like a feathered heart.
My mouth is a chisel, my hands
the crimes done by hands.

I sit in the forest talking of death
which is monotonous:
though there are many ways of dying
there is only one death song,
the colour of mist:
it says Why Why

I do not want revenge, I do not want expiation,
I only want to ask someone
how I was lost,
how I was lost

I am the lost heart of a murderer
who has not yet killed,
who does not yet know he wishes
to kill; who is still the same
as the others

I am looking for him,
he will have answers for me,
he will watch his step, he will be
cautious and violent, my claws
will grow through his hands
and become claws, he will not be caught.

Ingeborg Bachmann

Ingeborg Bachmann was born in 1926 in Klagenfurt, Austria, and grew up in the valley town of Carinthia. She studied philosophy and law at Innsbruck and Grak, receiving her doctorate from the University of Vienna. Her dissertation was on the existentialism of German philosopher Martin Heidegger. She worked as a producer for a Viennese radio station until 1953, lived in Italy for four years, and studied at Harvard College in 1955. In 1959 and 1960 Bachmann gave a series of lectures at Frankfurt University concerning the existential situation of the modern writer. She lived and worked intermittently in Munich, Paris, Vienna, and other European cities until her 1973 death in Rome during a hotel fire.

Bachmann's first book of verse, *Borrowed Time*, appeared in 1953, followed by a second collection, *Invocation of the Great Bear*, in 1956. She also wrote radio plays, opera libretti, the novel *Malina* (1972), and a book of stories translated into English with the title *The Thirteenth Year* (1964). Still she is best known for her poetry and is considered one of the finest postwar German-language poets. Her poems are highly philosophical, literate, and complex, containing numerous allusions to western literature. But they are also passionate and contemplative, questioning the reality of love and human relationships.

Fog Land

In winter my loved one retires
to live with the beasts of the forest.
That I must be back before morning
the vixen knows well, and she laughs.
Now the low clouds quiver! And down
on my upturned collar there falls
a landslide of brittle ice.

In winter my loved one retires,
a tree among trees, and invites
the crows in their desolation
into her beautiful boughs. She knows
that as soon as night falls the wind
lifts her stiff, hoar-frost-embroidered
evening gown, sends me home.

In winter my loved one retires,
a fish among fishes, and dumb.
Slave to the waters she ripples
with her fins' gentle motion within,
I stand on the bank and look down
till ice floes drive me away,
her dipping and turning hidden.

And stricken again by the blood-cry
of the bird that tautens his wings
over my head, I fall down
on the open field; she is plucking
the hens, and she throws me a whitened
collar bone. This round my neck,
off I go through the bitter down.

My loved one, I know, is unfaithful,
and sometimes she stalks and she hovers

on high-heeled shoes to the city
and deeply in bars with her straw
will kiss the lips of the glasses,
and finds words for each and for all.
But this language is alien to me.

It is fog land I have seen,
It is fog heart I have eaten.

(Michael Hamburger, tr.)

Exile

A dead man I am who travels
not registered anywhere
unknown in the realm of prefects
redundant in the golden cities
and in the countryside's green

written off long ago
and provided with nothing

Only with wind with time and with sound

who cannot live among human beings

I with the German language
this cloud around me
that I keep as a house
drive through all languages

Oh, how it darkens
those muted those rain tones
only few of them fall

Up into brighter zones it will carry the dead man

(Michael Hamburger, tr.)

Curriculum Vitae

Long is the night,
long as the shame of the man
who can't manage to die, long
under the lamp post his naked
eye swung, and his eye, blind with the breath of gin
and the smell of a blonde girl's wet flesh
under his nails, oh God, long is the night.

My hair won't turn white,
for I dropped from a womb of machines,
Rose Red smeared tar on my forehead
and curls, they had
strangled her snow-white sister. But I,
the oldest, marched through a town
of ten hundred thousand souls, and my foot
stepped on a soul-louse under the leather sky from which
ten hundred thousand peace-pipes
were hanging, mutely. And often
I wish for angels' repose
and hunting grounds, sick
of the powerless cries
of my friends.

With wide-straddling legs and wings,
youth like some marsh grass shot up
over me, over ordure, over jasmine it went
on those towering nights with their square-
root dilemmas, breathing
the wisdom of death on my window each hour,
giving me wolf's milk, and pouring
old age's ridicule into my throat,
when I fell
over folios in sleep,
in a disconcerting dream
where I wasn't found worthy of thought,
playing with tassels
whose fringes were snakes.

And our mothers would also
dream of the future of their men,
they would see someone powerful,
revolutionary, withdrawn,
and mostly after prayers in the garden,
while bending over the burning weeds,
hand in hand with the howling child
of their love. Oh my gloomy father,
why were you always so silent then,
nor ever thought past tomorrow?

Forsaken in the fire fountains,
a night of crouching near a gun
that misses fire, so goddamn long
a night, under the refuse
of a jaundiced moon, whose light
stunk gall, there rumbled in the shadow
of a dream of power (why hide it now?)
the bobsled of our ornamented
past, and cut me down.
Not that I slept: awake
under the icy bones I trailed it

homeward, wrapped my arms and legs
in ivy and daubed the ruins
white with droppings from the sun.
I kept the holy festivals,
and only after prayers
did bread appear.

In a self-righteous decade
a man moves faster from one light
to another, from one country
to another, under the rainbow,
the compass points stuck in his heart,
towards the radius labeled the night.
Wide open. From the mountains
one sees oceans, in the oceans
mountains, and where the clouds line up
in pews, the swinging of the bells
of the one and only world. Which world
I was commanded not to know.

It happened on a Friday—
my life ran down with fasting,
the air oozed with vapors of lemon
and the fishbone stuck in my craw—
when out of the gutted fish, I lifted
a ring which, thrown away at the time
of my birth, fell in the river
of night, where it sank.
I threw it back to the night.

O if I had no fear of death!
If I had the word
(nor knew its loss)
if I had no thorns within my heart
(but battered out the sun)
If I had no greed within my mouth
(nor drank from the wild water)

if I waited without blinking
(nor saw the threads before me).
Must they drag the sky away?
Let the Earth not play me false,
but lay me long in stillness,
long in stillness, for Night
with its black snout to nose me,
and dream the next caress
of its devouring arms.

(Jerome Rothenberg, tr.)

Louise Bogan

Louise Bogan was born in 1897 in Livermore Falls, Maine. Because her parents had financial as well as marital problems, her childhood was not a happy one. In 1909 the family moved to Boston, and Bogan entered the Girl's Latin School where she studied Greek, Latin, and classical versification. It was there that she began to write poetry. She enrolled in Boston University in 1915 and considered attending Radcliffe College the next year but decided instead to marry Curt Alexander, a professional soldier. Later she admitted that this marriage was not a happy one and that she had undertaken it partly to escape her troubled home life. Bogan gave birth to a daughter before leaving Alexander in 1919.

Bogan was drawn to the bohemian life of Greenwich Village, and when Alexander died she used the pension money he left her to settle there. She became friends with William Carlos Williams, Margaret Mead, Edmund Wilson, as well as other renowned figures, and she continued to write poetry. Her first book of poems, *Body of This Death*, appeared in 1923 and was followed by *Dark Summer* in 1929. Bogan married for a second time in 1925, to Raymond Holden, a minor novelist and member of a prominent family. After this marriage ended in 1934, Bogan began a relationship with poet Theodore Roethke; this lasted until his death in 1963.

Bogan had been the poetry editor of *The New Yorker* from 1931 until 1969. Later volumes of her poetry include *The Sleeping Fury* (1937), *Poems and New Poems* (1941), and *The Blue Estuaries: Poems 1923-1968* (1968). Some of her essays about other poets were printed in *Selected Criticism* (1955). Unlike many of her friends, Bogan was not a part of the social activist movements of the thirties. She believed that humanity's hope lay in the transformation of the individual spirit. This reliance on inner strength is evident in much of her work, which expresses passionate emotions in a controlled, classical form. A recipient of many poetry prizes, she served as visiting professor and writer-in-residence at such institutions as Brandeis University and the University of Washington. Bogan died in 1970.

A Tale

This youth too long has heard the break
Of waters in a land of change.
He goes to see what suns can make
From soil more indurate and strange.

He cuts what holds his days together
And shuts him in, as lock on lock:
The arrowed vane announcing weather,
The tripping racket of a clock;

Seeking, I think, a light that waits
Still as a lamp upon a shelf,—
A land with hills like rocky gates
Where no sea leaps upon itself.

But he will find that nothing dares
To be enduring, save where, south
Of hidden deserts, torn fire glares
On beauty with a rusted mouth,—

Where something dreadful and another
Look quietly upon each other.

Portrait

She has no need to fear the fall
Of harvest from the laddered reach
Of orchards, nor the tide gone ebbing
    From the steep beach.

Nor hold to pain's effrontery
Her body's bulwark, stern and savage,
Nor be a glass, where to foresee
    Another's ravage.

What she has gathered, and what lost,
She will not find to lose again.
She is possessed by time, who once
    Was loved by men.

Winter Swan

It is a hollow garden, under the cloud;
Beneath the heel a hollow earth is turned;
Within the mind the live blood shouts aloud;
Under the breast the willing blood is burned,
Shut with the fire passed and the fire returned.
But speak, you proud!
Where lies the leaf-caught world once thought abiding,
Now but a dry disarray and artifice?
Here, to the ripple cut by the cold, drifts this
Bird, the long throat bent back, and the eyes in hiding.

Girl's Song

Winter, that is a fireless room
In a locked house, was our love's home.
The days turn, and you are not here,
O changing with the little year!

Now when the scent of plants half-grown
Is more the season's than their own
And neither sun nor wind can stanch
The gold forsythia's dripping branch,—

Another maiden, still not I,
Looks from some hill upon some sky,
And, since she loves you, and she must,
Puts her young cheek against the dust.

Late

The cormorant still screams
Over cave and promontory.
Stony wings and bleak glory
Battle in your dreams.
Now sullen and deranged,
Not simply, as a child,
You look upon the earth
And find it harrowed and wild.
Now, only to mock
At the sterile cliff laid bare,
At the cold pure sky unchanged,
You look upon the rock,

You look upon the air.

Song for a Slight Voice

If ever I render back your heart
So long to me delight and plunder,
It will be bound with the firm strings
That men have built the viol under.

Your stubborn, piteous heart, that bent
To be the place where music stood,
Upon some shaken instrument
Stained with the dark of resinous blood,

Will find its place, beyond denial,
Will hear the dance, O be most sure,
Laid on the curved wood of the viol
Or on the struck tambour.

Spirit's Song

How well you served me above ground,
Most truthful sight, firm-builded sound.

And how you throve through hunger, waste,
Sickness and health, informing taste;

And smell, that did from dung and heather,
Corruption, bloom, mix well together.

But you, fierce delicate tender touch,
Betrayed and hurt me overmuch,

For whom I lagged with what a crew
O far too long, and poisoned through!

Gwendolyn Brooks

Gwendolyn Brooks was born in 1917 in Topeka, Kansas, but grew up in Chicago, Illinois, where she began writing poetry at the age of seven. In 1936 she graduated from Wilson Junior College. During the thirties she was publicity director for the NAACP Youth Council in Chicago, and during the early forties she entered a poetry workshop at the South Side Community Art Center to study modernist poetry. She married Henry Blakely in 1939; they had two children.

In the tradition of such Harlem Renaissance poets as Langston Hughes and Countee Cullen, Brooks combines jazz rhythms and street slang with formal poetic conventions. Her first book, *A Street in Bronzeville* (1945), has long since become a classic. In 1950, for her second volume, *Annie Allen* (1949), Brooks received the Pulitzer Prize for Poetry. It was the first time the prestigious award was given to a black author. The books that followed, *Bronzeville Boys and Girls* (1956) and *The Bean Eaters* (1960), are consistent with the others in theme, featuring characters much like the people she knew while growing up in Chicago. Her novel, *Maud Martha* (1953), is a story of a black girl's coming of age, which in terms of its subject was highly innovative for its time.

Although Brooks had been writing about black characters from the start, she was challenged by a group of young black poets at a conference at Fisk University in 1967 to politicize her commitment to black culture. Instead of merely using blacks as the subjects of her writing, she was inspired to direct her works "to all manner of blacks." Soon after, she began teaching a poetry-writing workshop designed for Chicago's black youth. Her later collections, including *In the Mecca* (1968), *Riot* (1969), *Beckonings* (1975), and *To Disembark* (1981), are further evidence of her dedication. She has also written an autobiography, *Report from Part One* (1979), in addition to several books of poetry for children.

Brooks was the first black woman poet to achieve such widespread recognition. Through several decades of writing, her eloquent and natural use of language as well as her skill at characterization has made her one of the few poets who is appreciated both critically and popularly.

A Song in the Front Yard

I've stayed in the front yard all my life.
I want a peek at the back
Where it's rough and untended and hungry weed grows.
A girl gets sick of a rose.

I want to go in the back yard now
And maybe down the alley,
To where the charity children play.
I want a good time today.

They do some wonderful things.
They have some wonderful fun.
My mother sneers, but I say it's fine
How they don't have to go in at quarter to nine.
My mother, she tells me that Johnnie Mae
Will grow up to be a bad woman.
That George'll be taken to Jail soon or late
(On account of last winter he sold our back gate.)

But I say it's fine. Honest, I do.
And I'd like to be a bad woman, too,
And wear the brave stockings of night-black lace

And strut down the streets with paint on my face.

The Murder

This is where poor Percy died,
Short of the age of one,
His brother Brucie, with a grin,
Burned him up for fun.

No doubt, poor Percy watched the fire
Chew on his baby dress
With sweet delight, enjoying too
His brother's happiness.

No doubt, poor Percy looked around
And wondered at the heat,
Was worried, wanted Mother,
Who gossiped down the street.

No doubt, poor shrieking Percy died
Loving Brucie still,
Who could, with clean and open eye,
Thoughtfully kill.

Brucie has no playmates now,
His mother mourns his lack.
Brucie keeps on asking, "When
Is Percy comin' back?"

Strong Men, Riding Horses
Lester after the western

Strong Men, riding horses. In the West
On a range five hundred miles. A Thousand. Reaching
From dawn to sunset. Rested blue to orange.
From hope to crying. Except that Strong Men are
Desert-eyed. Except that Strong Men are
Pasted to stars already. Have their cars
Beneath them. Rentless, too. Too broad of chest
To shrink when the Rough Man hails. Too flailing
To redirect the Challenger, when the challenge
Nicks; slams; buttonholes. Too saddled.

I am not like that. I pay rent, am addled
By illegible landlords, run, if robbers call.

What mannerisms I present, employ,
Are camouflage, and what my mouths remark
To word-wall off that broadness of the dark
Is pitiful.
I am not brave at all.

We Real Cool
The Pool Players.
Seven at the Golden Shovel.

We real cool. We
Left school. We

Lurk late. We
Strike straight. We

Sing sin. We
Thin gin. We

Jazz June. We
Die soon.

Mrs. Small

Mrs. Small went to the kitchen for her pocketbook
And came back to the living room with a peculiar look
And the coffee pot.
Pocketbook. Pot.
Pot. Pocketbook.

The insurance man was waiting there
With superb and cared-for hair.
His face did not have much time.
He did not glance with sublime
Love upon the little plump tan woman
With the half-open mouth and the half-mad eyes
And the smile half-human

Who stood in the middle of the living-room floor planning
   apple pies
And graciously offering him a steaming coffee pot.
Pocketbook. Pot.

"Oh!" Mrs. Small came to her senses,
Peered earnestly through thick lenses,
Jumped terribly. This, too, was a mistake,
Unforgivable no matter how much she had to bake.
For there can be no whiter whiteness than this one:
An insurance man's shirt on its morning run.
This Mrs. Small now soiled
With a pair of brown
Spurts (just recently boiled)
Of the "very best coffee in town."

"The best coffee in town is what *you* make, Delphine! There
   is none dandier!"
Those were the words of the pleased Jim Small—
Who was no bandier of words at all.
Jim Small was likely to give you a good swat
When he was *not*
Pleased. He was, absolutely, no bandier.

"I don't know where my mind is this morning,"
Said Mrs. Small, scorning
Apologies! For there was so much
For which to apologize! Oh such
Mountains of things, she'd never get anything done
If she begged forgiveness for each one.

She paid him.

But apologies and her hurry would not mix.
The six
Daughters were a-yell, a-scramble, in the hall. The four
Sons (horrors) could not be heard any more.

No.
The insurance man would have to glare
Idiotically into her own sterile stare
A moment—then depart,
Leaving her to release her heart
And dizziness
And silence her six
And mix
Her spices and core
And slice her apples, and find her four.
Continuing her part
Of the world's business.

Jessie Mitchell's Mother

Into her mother's bedroom to wash the ballooning body.
"My mother is jelly-hearted and she has a brain of jelly:
Sweet, quiver-soft, irrelevant. Not essential.
Only a habit would cry if she should die.
A pleasant sort of fool without the least iron...
Are you better, mother, do you think it will come today?"
The stretched yellow rag that was Jessie Mitchell's mother
Reviewed her. Young, and so thin, and so straight.
So straight! as if nothing could ever bend her.
But poor men would bend her, and doing things with poor
    men,
Being much in bed, and babies would bend her over,
And the rest of things in life that were for poor women,
Coming to them grinning and pretty with intent to bend
    and to kill.
Comparisons shattered her heart, ate at her bulwarks:
The shabby and the bright: she, almost hating her

daughter,
Crept into an old sly refuge: "Jessie's black
And her way will be black, and jerkier even than mine.
Mine, in fact, because I was lovely, had flowers
Tucked in the jerks, flowers were here and there..."
She revived for the moment settled and dried-up triumphs,
Forced perfume into old petals, pulled up the droop,
Refueled
Triumphant long-exhaled breaths.
Her exquisite yellow youth...

A Sunset of the City
Kathleen Eileen

Already I am no longer looked at with lechery or love.
My daughters and sons have put me away with marbles
      and dolls,
Are gone from the house.
My husband and lovers are pleasant or somewhat polite
And night is night.

It is a real chill out,
The genuine thing.
I am not deceived, I do not think it is still summer
Because sun stays and birds continue to sing.

It is summer-gone that I see, it is summer-gone.
The sweet flowers indrying and dying down,
The grasses forgetting their blaze and consenting to
      brown.

It is a real chill out. The fall crisp comes.

I am aware there is winter to heed.
There is no warm house
That is fitted with my need.

I am cold in this cold house this house
Whose washed echoes are tremulous down lost halls.
I am a woman, and dusty, standing among new affairs.
I am a woman who hurries through her prayers.

Tin intimations of a quiet core to be my
Desert and my dear relief
Come: there shall be such islanding from grief,
And small communion with the master shore.
Twang they. And I incline this ear to tin,
Consult a dual dilemma. Whether to dry
In humming pallor or to leap and die.

Somebody muffed it? Somebody wanted to joke.

To a Winter Squirrel

That is the way God made you.
And what is wrong with it? Why, nothing.
Except that you are cold and cannot cook.

Merdice can cook. Merdice
of murdered heart and docked sarcastic soul,
Merdice
the bolted nomad, on a winter noon
cooks guts; and sits in gas. (She has no shawl, her
            landlord has no coal.)

You out beyond the shellac of her look
and of her sill!
She envies you your furry
buffoonery
that enfolds your silver skill.
She thinks you are a mountain and a star, unbaffleable;
with sentient twitch and scurry.

Nina Cassian

Nina Cassian was born in 1924 in Galati, Rumania. She studied at the University of Bucharest and the Conservatory of Music; she is a composer and musician as well as a poet, translator, and author of children's literature. Cassian is regarded as one of the most distinctive and intelligent voices in contemporary Rumanian poetry. Her works include *On the Scale of One to One* (1947), *Selected Poems* (1955), *Discipline of the Harp* (1964), and *Lottery Poems* (1972).

Hills Picking Up the Moonlight

hills picking up the
moonlight like
huge sheep of stone
leaping heads huddled
in the hard freeze and sparkle

the moon then comes to me
builds me up
plasters me up
smashes my forehead
the moon

(Stavros Deligiorgis, tr.)

A Man

While fighting for his country, he lost an arm
and was suddenly afraid:
'From now on, I shall only be able to do things by
                                            halves.
I shall reap half a harvest.
I shall be able to play either the tune
or the accompaniment on the piano,
but never both parts together.
I shall be able to bang with only one fist
on doors, and worst of all
I shall only be able to half hold
my love close to me.
There will be things I cannot do at all,
applaud for example,
at shows where everyone applauds.'

From that moment on, he set himself to do
everything with twice as much enthusiasm.
And where the arm had been torn away
a wing grew.

(Roy MacGregor-Hastie, tr.)

Self-Portrait

However much I try, I will always be just what I am.
I will never be able to make my mouth rounder,
nor my eyes almond-shaped, nor my nose retroussé,
nor will I ever be able to change the shape of my skull.

For it is my lot to have this odd, triangular face,
rather like a sugar-loaf sometimes
or the prow of a pirate felucca,
and I shall always have this long hair, the colour of smoke.

It is my lot to walk this shape of mine about
aggressively, night and day,
wounding the retinae of those around me
when the image of my incongruity projects itself on walls.

To whom do I belong? My parents and grandparents have
rejected me
as have all races, black, brown, yellow and red
in temporary alliance in this. No species
is prepared to recognise me as one of its own.

It is only when I hurt myself and cry,
it is only when the cold bites deep,
it is only when time leaves a scar on me
that they say: Pretty. But I say: Human.

(Roy MacGregor-Hastie, tr.)

Rosario Castellanos

Rosario Castellanos was born in Mexico City in 1925 and grew up in the small Mexican town of Comitán, near the Guatemalan border. What she saw there of the lives of the Indians was to have a profound influence on her work. After studying philosophy at the University of Mexico and in Madrid, she worked for a time at the Indian Institutes in Chiapas and Mexico City. In later years, when she had established herself as a distinguished Mexican writer, she served as Mexico's ambassador to Israel. She was killed by a faulty electrical connection in a Tel Aviv hotel room in 1974.

Perhaps better known as a novelist, Rosario Castellanos is still Mexico's most important twentieth century woman poet. She began writing poetry at the age of fifteen. Eventually she was able to make her living as a writer, a rare feat for Mexican women. Her works include two novels, three collections of short stories, essays and criticisms, plays, and twelve books of poetry. Anger and anguish are the dominant tones in her poetry, which often exposes various forms of social oppression. *Looking at the Mona Lisa*, a book of her poetry, was translated into English by Maureen Ahern and was published in 1981.

Silence Near an Ancient Stone

I'm sitting here with all my words intact
like a basket of green fruit.

The fragments
of a thousand ancient and defeated gods
seek and bind each other in my blood, straining
to rebuild their statue.
From their shattered mouths
a song struggles to rise to mine,
an aroma of burnt resin, some gesture
of mysterious carved stone.
But I am oblivion, betrayal,
the shell that did not hold an echo
from even the smallest wave in the sea.
I do not watch the submerged temples;
I watch only the trees moving their vast shadows
over the ruins, biting the passing wind
with acid teeth.
And the signs close beneath my eyes like
a flower under the awkward fingers of the blind.
Yet I know: behind
my body another body crouches,
and around me many breaths
cross furtively
like nocturnal animals in the jungle.
I know that in some place
the same
as the cactus in the desert,
a clustered heart of thorns, awaits a name
as the cactus does the rain.
But I know only as few words
in the language or the stone
beneath which they buried my ancestor alive.

(Maureen Ahern, tr.)

Empty House

I remember a house I left behind.
It's empty now.
Curtains blowing in the wind,
boards clapping stubbornly
against old walls.
In the garden where grass begins
to spill its borders,
through the rooms of covered furniture,
among the empty mirrors,
loneliness
glides and wanders
on silent velvet feet.

A girl grew up here,
her slim sad cypress body sprouted
where her footsteps have left their imprint
along the hollow silent corridor.

(Two braids stretching down her back
like twin guardian angels.
Her hands only knew how to
close windows.)

Grey adolescence, shadowy vocation,
a destiny of death:
the stairways sleep. A house
that could never hold you, collapses.

(Maureen Ahern, tr.)

Malinche

From the throne of command my mother said: "He is dead."
And threw herself
into the arms of another, usurper, stepfather
who didn't sustain her with the respect
a servant renders to the majesty of a queen
but groveled in their mutual shame
of lovers and accomplices.

From the Plaza of Enchange
my mother announced: "She is dead."

The scale
balanced for an instant
the chocolate bean lay motionless in the bin
the sun remained at mid-point in the sky
waiting the sign
which shot like an arrow
became the sharp wail of the mourners.

"The bloom of many petals was deflowered,
the perfume evaporated,
the torch flame burned out.

A girl returns to scratch up the earth
in the place
where the midwife buried her umbilicus.

She returns to the Place of Those Who Once Lived.

She recognizes her father assassinated,
ay, ay, ay, poison, a dagger,
a snare before his feet, a vine noose.

They take each other by the hand and walk, walk

disappearing into the fog."

Such were the wail and the lamentations
over an anonymous body: a corpse
that was not mine because I, sold
to the merchants, was on my way as a slave,
a nobody, into exile.

Cast out, expelled
from the kingdom, from the palace and from the warm belly
of her who bore me in legitimate marriage bed
who hated me because I was her equal
in stature and in rank
who saw herself in me and hating her image
dashed the mirror against the ground.

I advance toward destiny in chains
leaving behind all that I can still hear,
the funeral murmurs with which I am buried.

And the voice of my mother in tears—in tears!
she who decrees my death!

(Maureen Ahern, tr.)

Home Economics

This is the golden rule, the secret of order:
a place for everything
and everything in its place. That's how I've fixed my house.

An impeccable bookstand:
one shelf for the novels,
another for essays
and poetry on all the others

If you open a closet it smells of lavender
and you can't mistake the linen tablecloths
for the ones for daily use.

There's also the set of china for special occasions
and the other one that's used, broken, mismatched
and is never complete.

The clothes are in the right drawers
and the furniture is properly arranged
to make the room harmonious.

Naturally the tops
(of everything) are polished and clean.
It's also natural
that dust isn't hiding in the corners.

But there are some things I just put down here or there
or toss in the place I keep for catchalls.

A few things. A cry, for example,
that was never cried,
a distracting nostalgia,
an ache, a pain whose name was blotted out,
a vow never kept, an anguish

that evaporated like perfume in
a partially closed bottle.

And remnants of time lost anywhere.

This discourages me. I always say, tomorrow...
and then forget. And proudly show company
a room that shines with the golden rule
my mother gave me.

(Maureen Ahern, tr.)

Kamala Das

Kamala Das was born in 1934 to an upper-class family in Malabar, South India. Her mother, Balamani Amma, had also been a poet. Das was educated privately, and at age fifteen she married a banker, K. Madhava Das. They had three sons.

Das, who writes extensively in English, is known for poetry that explores topics considered taboo for Indian women writers of her social class. Her poetry collections include *Summer in Calcutta: Fifty Poems* (1965), *The Descendants* (1967), and *The Old Playhouse and Other Poems* (1973). She has also written a novel, *Alphabet of Lust* (1977), several volumes of short stories, and an autobiography, *My Story* (1978), which has been translated into eleven languages.

My Son's Teacher

My son is four. His teacher swooned on a
                              grey pavement
Five miles from here and died. From where she
                              lay, her new skirt
Flapped and fluttered, a green flag, half-mast,
                              to proclaim death's
Minor triumph. The wind was strong, the poor
                              men carried
Pink elephant-gods to the sea that day. They
                              moved in
Long gaudy processions, they clapped cymbals,

they beat drums
and they sang aloud. She who lay in a faint
was drowned
In their song. The evening paper carried the
news. He
Bathed, drank milk, wrote two crooked lines of
Ds and waited.
But the dead rang no doorbell. He is only four,
For many years he will not be told that tragedy
Flew over him one afternoon, an old sad bird, and
Gently touched his shoulder with its wing.

Summer in Calcutta

What is this drink but
The April sun, squeezed
Like an orange in
My glass? I sip the
Fire. I drink and drink
Again. I am drunk,
Again. I am drunk,
Yes, but on the gold
Of suns. What noble
Venom now flows through
My veins and fills my
Mind with unhurried
Laughter? My worries
Doze. Wee bubbles ring
My glass, like a bride's
Nervous smile, and meet
My lips.
Dear, forgive

This moment's lull in
Wanting you, the blur
In memory. How
Brief the term of my
Devotion, how brief
Your reign when I with
Glass in hand, drink, drink
And drink again this
Juice of April suns.

The Wilderness

Once I thought I belonged to people like my father
Mother sister husband
Then I thought myself my lover's
And later as I grew,
For certain I knew
That only my readers needed me.
Today I am lost, I doubt if anyone
Needs me at all.
This paper is white wilderness
And my cries are silent.

There is nobody with me. . .
I am what they once called Kamala.

A Request

When I die
Do not throw the meat and bones away
But pile them up
And
Let them tell
By their smell
What life was worth
On this earth
What love was worth
In the end.

A Holiday for Me

Merciful and blue are the mountains I go to climb
For my first lone holiday
Hills of cerulean blue that I shall climb like a breeze
On my first lone holiday
The only mountain ranges left for me
For a great lone holiday
I shall leave all the heavy luggage behind
Shall leave two teddy-bears and a child

My blindness shall take care of the senders-off
My deafness of the wailing
I shall carry with me only a laugh
I shall travel as light as I can.

Noémia de Sousa

Noémia de Sousa was born in Lourenço Marques, Mozambique, in 1927 and attended secondary school in Brazil. She lived for a time in Lisbon, Portugal, and protested the Portuguese government's domination of Mozambique. Because of her political activities, she was forced to leave Portugal in 1964. She moved to Paris and wrote under the pseudonym Vera Micaia. De Sousa, who writes in Portuguese, was the first black African woman to attain an international reputation as a poet.

If You Want To Know Me

If you want to know me
examine with careful eyes
this bit of black wood
which some unknown Makonde brother
cut and carved
with his inspired hands
in the distant lands of the North.

This is what I am
empty sockets despairing of possessing life
a mouth torn open in an anguished wound
huge hands outspread
and raised in imprecation and in threat
a body tattooed with wounds seen and unseen
from the harsh whipstrokes of slavery
tortured and magnificent

proud and mysterious
Africa from head to foot
This is what I am.

If you want to understand me
come, bend over this soul of Africa
in the black dockworker's groans
the Chope's frenzied dances
the Changanas' rebellion
in the strange sadness which flows
from an African song, through the night.

And ask no more
to know me
for I'm nothing but a shell of flesh
where Africa's revolt congealed
its cry pregnant with hope.

(Margaret Dickinson, tr.)

The Poem of João

João was young like us
João had wideawake eyes
and alert ears
hands reaching forwards
a mind cast for tomorrow
a mouth to cry an eternal "no"
João was young like us

João enjoyed art and literature
enjoyed poetry and Jorge Amado

enjoyed books of meat and soul
which breathe life, struggle, sweat and hope
João dreamt of Zambezi's flowing books spreading culture
for mankind, for the young, our brothers
João fought that books might be for all
João loved literature
João was young like us

João was the father, the mother, the brother of multitudes
João was the blood and the sweat of multitudes
and suffered and was happy like the multitudes
He smiled that same tired smile of shop girls leaving work
he suffered with the passivity of the peasant women
he felt the sun piercing like a thorn in the Arabs' midday
he bargained on bazaar benches with the Chinese
he sold tired green vegetables with the Asian traders
he howled spirituals from Harlem with Marion Anderson
he swayed to the Chope marimbas on a Sunday
he cried out with the rebels their cry of blood
he was happy in the caress of the manioc-white moon
he sang with the shibalos their songs of homesick longing
and he hoped with the same intensity of all
for dazzling dawns with open mouths
to sing
João was the blood and sweat of multitudes
João was young like us.

João and Mozambique were intermingled
João would not have been João without Mozambique
João was like a palm tree, a coconut palm
a piece of rock, a Lake Niassa, a mountain
an Incomati, a forest, a maçala tree
a beach, a Maputo, an Indian Ocean
João was an integral and deep rooted part of Mozambique
João was young like us.

João longed to live and longed to conquer life

that is why he loathed prisons, cages, bars
and loathed the men who make them.
For João was free
João was an eagle born to fly
João loathed prisons and the men who make them
João was young like us.

And because João was young like us
and had wideawake eyes
and enjoyed art and poetry and Jorge Amado
and was the blood and sweat of multitudes
and was intermingled with Mozambique
and was an eagle born to fly
and hated prisons and the men who make them
Ah, because of all this we have lost João
We have lost João.

Ah, this is why we have lost João
why we weep night and day for João
for João whom they have stolen from us.

And we ask
But why have they taken João,
João who was young and ardent like us
João who thirsted for life
João who was brother to us all
why have they stolen from us João
who spoke of hope and dawning days
João whose glance was like a brother's hug
João who always had somewhere for one of us to stay
João who was our mother and our father
João who would have been our saviour
João whom we loved and love
João who belongs so surely to us
oh, why have they stolen João from us?
and no one answers
indifferent, no one answers.

But we know
why they took João from us
João, so truly our brother.

But what does it matter?
They think they have stolen him but João is here with us
is here in others who will come
in others who have come.
For João is not alone
João is a multitude
João is the blood and the sweat of multitudes
and João, in being João, is also Joaquim, José
Abdullah, Fang, Mussumbuluco, is Mascarenhas
Omar, Yutang, Fabiao
João is the multitude, the blood and sweat of multitudes

And who will take José, Joaquim, Abdullah
Fang, Mussumbuluco, Mascarenhas, Omar, Fabiao?
Who?
Who will take us all and lock us in a cage?
Ah, they have stolen João from us
But João is us all.
Because of this João hasn't left us
and João "was" not, he "is" and "will be".
For João is us all, we are a multitude
and the multitude
who can take the multitude and lock it in a cage?

(Margaret Dickinson, tr.)

Hilda Doolittle ("H.D.")

Hilda Doolittle, the only sister to five brothers, was born in Bethlehem, Pennsylvania, in 1886. Her father was Charles Doolittle, a professor of mathematics and astronomy at Lehigh University. Her mother, Helen Wolle Doolittle, was an active member of the mystic Protestant sect, the Moravian Brotherhood. The family moved to Wycote, a suburb of Philadelphia in 1895. H.D. entered Bryn Mawr College in 1904 but left two years later due to poor health. However, influenced by her friend (and former fiancé), Ezra Pound, she continued to read heavily on her own and to write poems and articles for newspapers and journals.

In 1911 Pound brought H.D. to London where he was already established. He introduced her to such literary figures as Ford Maddox Ford, William Butler Yeats, F.S. Flint, and Richard Aldington. It was Pound who first referred to the poet by her initials on that famous occasion in the tea room of the British Museum in 1912 when he signed a group of her poems "H.D. Imagiste." Pound believed her early poems represented what he named "imagism," a movement that proposed to capture a concrete image without unnecessary words, symbolism, or the artificial imposition of rhymes and meters. This movement, which also included Amy Lowell and D.H. Lawrence, among others, was in part a reaction against the profuse imagery and sentimentality characteristic of most nineteenth-century poetry. H.D.'s first volume of verse, *Sea Garden*, was published in 1916. These poems are among the finest examples of imagist poetry.

In 1913, H.D. married Richard Aldington, but she soon endured a series of misfortunes that lasted throughout World War I. Among them were a miscarriage in 1915, the loss of her brother Gilbert to the war in 1918, the death of her father soon after, her separation from

Aldington in 1919, and finally her serious bout with double pneumonia. She survived all of these calamities to give birth to her daughter, Perdita, in 1919. She had the support of her friend Winifred Ellerman (Bryher), the wealthy daughter of a shipping magnate and author of adventure novels, who also paid for the publication of H.D's second volume of poetry, *Hymen*, in 1921. The two women became lifelong friends and traveled together throughout Europe and America during the twenties.

With the publication of *Collected Poems* in 1925, H.D.'s reputation was established. She moved to Switzerland where she produced works that showed a widening range, although she continued to use classical settings. Her next book of poems, *Red Roses for Bronze*, was published in 1929, following the fiction pieces *Palimpsest* (1926) and *Hedylus* (1928), as well as the play *Hippolytus Temporizes* (1927). During 1933 and 1934 she underwent psychoanalysis in Vienna with Sigmund Freud and recounts that experience in *Tribute to Freud* (1956).

H.D. lived in London during World War II, writing the verse epic *Trilogy* between the years 1944 through 1946. Made up of three books, *The Walls Do Not Fall, Tribute to the Angels,* and *The Flowering of the Rod,* H.D. transforms the ruined landscape of the city into a vision of regeneration and unity. In her final years, she produced *Helen of Troy* (1961), a combination of poetry and prose that revises the story of Helen's abduction from Greece. In 1960, on her last trip to America, H.D. became the first woman to receive the Award of Merit Medal for Poetry given by the American Academy of Arts and Letters. She died in 1961 of a heart attack.

Sea Rose

Rose, harsh rose,
marred and with stint of petals,
meagre flower, thin,
sparse of leaf,

more precious
than a wet rose
single on a stem—
you are caught in the drift.

Stunted, with small leaf,
you are flung on the sand,
you are lifted
in the crisp sand
that drives in the wind.

Can the spice-rose
drip such acrid fragrance
hardened in a leaf?

The Wind Sleepers

Whiter
than the crust
left by the tide,
we are stung by the hurled sand
and the broken shells.

We no longer sleep
in the wind—
we awoke and fled
through the city gate.

Tear—
tear us an altar,
tug at the cliff-boulders,
pile them with the rough stones—
we no longer
sleep in the wind,
propitiate us.

Chant in a wail
that never halts,
pace a circle and pay tribute
with a song.

When the roar of a dropped wave
breaks into it,
pour meted words
of sea-hawks and gulls
and sea-birds that cry
discords.

Cities

Can we believe—by an effort
comfort our hearts:
it is not waste all this,
not placed here in disgust,
street after street,
each patterned alike,
no grace to lighten
a single house of the hundred
crowded into one garden-space.

Crowded—can we believe,
not in utter disgust,
in ironical play—
but the maker of cities grew faint
with the beauty of temple
and space before temple,
arch upon perfect arch,
of pillars and corridors that led out
to strange court-yards and porches
where sun-light stamped
hyacinth-shadows
black on the pavement.

That the maker of cities grew faint
with the splendour of palaces,
paused while the incense-flowers
from the incense-trees
dropped on the marble-walk,
thought anew, fashioned this—
street after street alike.

For alas,
he had crowded the city so full
that men could not grasp beauty.

beauty was over them,
through them, about them,
no crevice unpacked with the honey,
rare, measureless.

So he built a new city,
ah can we believe, not ironically
but for new splendour
constructed new people
to lift through slow growth
to a beauty unrivalled yet—
and created new cells,
hideous first, hideous now—
spread larvae across them,
not honey but seething life.

And in these dark cells,
packed street after street,
souls live, hideous yet—
O disfigured, defaced,
with no trace of the beauty
men once held so light.

Can we think a few old cells
were left—we are left—
grains of honey,
old dust of stray pollen
dull on our torn wings,
we are left to recall the old streets?

Is our task the less sweet
that the larvae still sleep in their cells?
Or crawl out to attack our frail strength:
You are useless. We live.
We await great events.
We are spread through this earth.
We protect our strong race.

You are useless.
Your cell takes the place
of our young future strength.

Though they sleep or wake to torment
and wish to displace our old cells—
thin rare gold—
that their larvae grow fat—
is our task the less sweet?

Though we wander about,
find no honey of flowers in this waste,
is our task the less sweet—
who recall the old splendour,
await the new beauty of cities?

The city is peopled
with spirits, not ghosts, O my love:

Though they crowded between
and usurped the kiss of my mouth
their breath was your gift,
their beauty, your life.

Orion Dead

(Artemis speaks.)

The cornel-trees
uplift from the furrows;
the roots at their bases
strike lower through the barley-sprays.

So arise and face me.
I am poisoned with rage of song.
I once pierced the flesh
of the wild deer,
now I am afraid to touch
the blue and the gold-veined hyacinths.

I will tear the full flowers
and the little heads
of the grape-hyacinths;
I will strip the life from the bulb
until the ivory layers
lie like narcissus petals
on the black earth.

Arise,
lest I bend an ash-tree
into a taut bow,
and slay—and tear
all the roots from the earth.

The cornel-wood blazes
and strikes through the barley-sprays
but I have lost heart for this.

I break a staff.
I break the tough branch.

I know no light in the woods.
I have lost pace with the wind.

The Walls Do Not Fall, Sel.

6

In me (the worm) clearly
is no righteousness, but this—

persistence; I escaped spider-snare,
bird-claw, scavenger bird-beak,

clung to grass-blade,
the back of a leaf

when storm-wind
tore it from its stem;

I escaped, I explored
rose-thorn forest,

was rain-swept
down the valley of a leaf;

was deposited on grass,
where mast by jewelled mast

bore separate ravellings
of encrusted gem-stuff

of the mist

from each banner-staff:

unintimidated by multiplicity
of magnified beauty,

such as your gorgon-great
dull eye can not focus

nor compass, I profit
by every calamity;

I eat my way out of it;
gorged on vine-leaf and mulberry,

parasite, I find nourishment:
when you cry in disgust,

a worm on the leaf,
a worm in the dust,

a worm on the ear-of-wheat,
I am yet unrepentant,

for I know how the Lord God
is about to manifest, when I,

the industrious worm,
spin my own shroud.

13

The Presence was spectrum-blue,
ultimate blue ray,

rare as radium, as healing;
my old self, wrapped round me,

was shroud (I speak of myself individually
but I was surrounded by companions

in this mystery);
do you wonder we are proud,

aloof,
indifferent to your good and evil?

peril, strangely encountered, strangely endured,
marks us;

we know each other
by secret symbols,

though, remote, speechless,
we pass each other on the pavement,

at the turn of the stair;
though no word pass between us,

there is subtle appraisement;
even if we snarl a brief greeting

or do not speak at all,
we know our Name,

we nameless initiates,
born of one mother,

companions
of the flame.

14

Yet we, the latter-day twice-born,
have our bad moments when

dragging the forlorn
husk of self after us,

we are forced to confess to
malaise and embarrassment;

we pull at this dead shell,
struggle but we must wait

till the new Sun dries off
the old-body humours;

awkwardly, we drag this stale
old will, old volition, old habit

about with us;
we are these people,

wistful, ironical, wilful,
who have no part in

new-world reconstruction,
in the confederacy of labour,

the practical issues of art
and the cataloguing of utilities:

O, do not look up
into the air,

you who are occupied
in the bewildering

sand-heap maze
of present-day endeavour;

you will be, not so much frightened

as paralysed with inaction,

and anyhow,
we have not crawled so very far

up our individual grass-blade
toward our individual star.

The Flowering of the Rod, Sel.

6

So I would rather drown, remembering—
than bask on tropic atolls

in the coral-seas; I would rather drown,
remembering—than rest on pine or fir-branch

where great stars pour down
their generating strength, Arcturus

or the sapphires of the Northern Crown;
I would rather beat in the wind, crying to these others

yours is the more foolish circling,
yours is the senseless wheeling

round and round—yours has no reason—
I am seeking heaven;

yours has no vision,
I see what is beneath me, what is above me,

what men say is-not—I remember,
I remember, I remember—you have forgot:

you think, even before it is half-over,
that your cycle is at an end,

but you repeat your foolish circling—again, again,
   again;
again, the steel sharpened on the stone;

again, the pyramid of skulls;
I gave pity to the dead,

O blasphemy, pity is a stone for bread,
only love is holy and love's ecstasy

that turns and turns and turns about one centre,
reckless, regardless, blind to reality,

that knows the Islands of the Blest are there,
for *many waters can not quench love's fire.*

7

Yet resurrection is a sense of direction,
resurrection is a bee-line,

straight to the horde and plunder,
the treasure, the store-room,

the honeycomb;
resurrection is remuneration,

food, shelter, fragrance
of myrrh and balm.

8

I am so happy,
I am the first or the last

of a flock or a swarm;
I am *full of new wine*;

I am branded with a word,
I am burnt with wood,

drawn from glowing ember,
not cut, not marked with steel;

I am the first or the last to renounce
iron, steel, metal;

I have gone forward,
I have gone backward,

I have gone onward from bronze and iron,
into the Golden Age.

9

No poetic phantasy
but a biological reality,

a fact: I am an entity
like bird, insect, plant

or sea-plant cell;
I live; I am alive;

take care, do not know me,
deny me, do not recognise me,

shun me; for this reality
is infectious—ecstasy.

10

It is no madness to say
you will fall, you great cities,

(now the cities lie broken);
it is not tragedy, prophecy

from a frozen Priestess,
a lonely Pythoness

who chants, who sings
in broken hexameters,

doom, doom to city-gates,
to rulers, to kingdoms;

it is simple reckoning, algebraic,
it is geometry on the wing,

not patterned, a gentian
in an ice-mirror,

yet it is, if you like, a lily
folded like a pyramid,

a flower-cone,
not a heap of skulls;

it is a lily, if you will,
each petal, a kingdom, an aeon,

and it is the seed of a lily
that having flowered,

will flower again;
it is that smallest grain,

the least of all seeds
that grows branches

where the birds rest;
it is that flowering balm,

it is heal-all,
everlàsting;

it is the greatest among herbs
and becometh a tree.

Carolyn Forché

Carolyn Forché was born in 1950 in Detroit, Michigan. Her father, a tool and die maker, is of Slovakian ancestry. Forché grew up in rural Michigan and, with her mother's encouragement, began to write poems at the age of nine. She received a B.A. in creative writing from Justin Morrill College of Michigan State University in 1972 and an M.F.A. from Bowling Green State University in 1975. She was a visiting lecturer in poetry at Justin Morrill in Spring 1974 and has been a visiting professor and writer at schools in New York and elsewhere. Forché was a journalist and human rights activist in El Salvador from 1978 to 1980, and she gives lectures on human rights as well as poetry readings.

Forché's first publication was the poem "Artisan Well," which appeared in *Ingenue* magazine in 1968. In 1976 her first book of poems, *Gathering the Tribes*, was published as part of the Yale Series of Younger Poets. *The Country Between Us* appeared in 1982. Forché translated into English, *Flowers from the Volcano* (1982), a book by El Salvadorean poet Claribel Alegría. She also wrote the text for *El Salvador: The Work of Thirty Photographers* (1983).

Forché's poetry expresses a sense of continuity that is unusual in contemporary poetry. Her poems connect the present to the past by the use of history and ritual. Her recent works have become more politicized due to the years spent witnessing the El Salvadorean War.

Early Night

I wrap myself in sheep leather,
kick heavy snow over its own tough skin.
Snow, daylight, ghosts in my mouth.

Here my round Slovak face feels like
whale meat on soapstone, I cannot
touch myself without screaming.
With a fist of Slavic I toss
old forgotten language to birds
asleep in flight, in snarling ice they stuff
their faces in their wings.

Hold to the wooden arms of bare oak.

I walk like this alone, old country
boots munching the field.
This snow is the snow of Urals
swarming upward, ashes, birds
frozen solid into stars.

Mountain Abbey, Surrounded by Elk Horns

Bells crack ice, white cattle
chew clean
red slopes that back away
from the mountain monastery.

Seventeen years of solitude is seventeen
years. Quiet. Punching eighty loaves of bread
a day, delivering
small cows.

Dawns thin out, like onion leaves,
each day's reading,
such pale paper
that it fills an open window.

Knowing dry feet of birds,
small sky between summits,
the swelling of animal mothers.

Each day, relived, a matter
of faith
that white cattle biting
sage of this hillside were not
already slaughtered.

The Island
For Claribel Alegría

1

In Deya when the mist
rises out of the rocks it comes
so close to her hands she could
tear it to pieces like bread.
She holds her drink and motions
with one hand to describe this:
what she would do with so many
baskets of bread.

Mi prieta, Asturias called her,
my dark little one. Neruda
used the word *negrita*, and it is
true: her eyes, her hair,
both violent, as black
as certain mornings have been
for the last fourteen years.
She wears a white cotton dress.
Tiny mirrors have been stitched
to it—when I look for myself
in her, I see the same face
over and over.

I have the fatty eyelids
of a Slavic factory girl,
the pale hair of mixed blood.
Although José Martí has said
we have lived our lives in the heart
of the beast, I have never heard
it pounding. When I have seen
an animal, I have never reached
for a knife. It is like

Americans to say it is only a bear
looking for something to eat
in the garbage.

But we are not unalike.
When we look at someone, we are seeing
someone else. When we listen
we hear something taking place
in the past. When I talk to her
I know what I will be saying
twenty years from now.

2

Last summer she returned
to Salvador again. It had been
ten years since *Ashes of Izalco*
was burned in a public place,
ten years without bushes
of coffee, since her eyes
crossed the finca like black
scattering birds.

It was simple. She was
there to embrace her mother.
As she walked through her village
the sight of her opened its windows.
It was simple. She had come
to flesh out the memory of a poet
whose body was never found.

Had it changed? It was different.
In Salvador nothing is changed.

3

Deya? A cluster of the teeth,

the bones of the world, greener
than Corsica. In English
you have no word for this. I can't
help you. I am safe here. I have
everything I could want.
In the morning I watch the peak
of the Teix knife into the clouds.
To my country I ship poetry instead
of bread, so I cut through nothing.
I give nothing, so you see I have
nothing, according to myself.

Deya has seven different shawls
of wind. The sky holds them
out to her, helps her into them.
I am *xaloc*, a wind
from the southwest as far away
as my country and there is nothing
to help me in or out of it.

Carolina, do you know how long it takes
any one voice to reach another?

Departure

We take it with us, the cry
of a train slicing a field
leaving its stiff suture, a distant
tenderness as when rails slip
behind us and our windows
touch the field, where it seems
the dead are awake and so reach
for each other. Your hand
cups the light of a match
to your mouth, to mine, and I want
to ask if the dead hold
their mouths in their hands like this
to know what is left of them.
Between us, a tissue of smoke,
a bundle of belongings, luggage
that will seem to float beside us,
the currency we will change
and change again. Here is the name
of a friend who will take you in,
the papers of a man who vanished,
the one you will become when
the man you have been disappears.
I am the woman whose photograph
you will not recognize, whose face
emptied your eyes, whose eyes
were brief, like the smallest
of cities we slipped through.

Gloria Fuertes

Gloria Fuertes was born in 1918 in Madrid, Spain, to working-class parents. She says that she began to recite her own poems before she could read. She attended university in Madrid and taught Spanish literature in the United States for three years. In Spain, Fuertes founded a series of readings by women poets and has given many readings of her own. She is also the founder of *Arquero*, a Spanish poetry review.

Fuertes' volumes include *Unknown Island* (1950), *I Advise You To Drink Thread* (1954), and *Selected Poetry* (1970). Her poetry is in touch with her working-class background, and she writes eloquently of the oppression of the poor in Spain—particularly the oppression of women. Fuertes has won prizes for her children's literature as well as for her poetry. A book of her poems, *Off the Map*, was translated into English and published in 1984.

Autobiography

At the foot of the Cathedral of Burgos
my mother was born.
At the foot of the Cathedral of Madrid
my father was born.
At the foot of my mother I was born
one afternoon in the middle of Spain.
My father was a worker,
my mother was a seamstress.
I wanted to take off with the circus
but I'm only what I am.
When I was little
I went to a reformatory and a free school.
As a kid I was sickly
and summered in a sanatorium,
but now I get around.
I've had at least seven love affairs,
some bad daddies,
and a marvelous appetite.
Now I've got two minor convictions
and a kiss from time to time.

(Philip Levine
and Ada Long, trs.)

It's Useless

It's useless at this date
to start punishing the rose and the bird,
useless to burn candles in the hallways,
useless to prohibit anything,
like speaking,
eating meat,
drinking books,
traveling for nothing on the streetcars,
desiring certain creatures,
smoking grass,
telling the truth,
loving your enemy,
it's a waste of time to prohibit anything.

There are announcements in the papers,
there are posters stuck on every corner
that prohibit the eating of fried birds,
but they never stop the roasting of men,
the eating of naked men with a gun's hunger.

Why are birds protected by those
who execute the seventh and fifth commandments?
Have they protected the Korean children?
Men go on eating them in white sauce.

The Patron of Animals is making a fool of herself.

Have they stopped the eating of innocent fish,
the pure and tender lambs,
the sad sea bass,
partridges?

And what can you say
about Mariquita Pérez

for whom expensive coats are bought
while there are girls without dolls or clothes?
The sick work,
the old exercise,
they sell heroin in all the bars,
teen-agers are for sale,
and all this goes on officially.
Get it straight, nobody does anything just because he's good-hearted.
You've got to go nuts and start screaming:
"As long as you murder, I'll eat fried birds!"

(Philip Levine
and Ada Long, trs.)

When I Hear Your Name

When I hear your name
I feel a little robbed of it;
it seems unbelievable
that half a dozen letters could say so much.

My compulsion is to blast down every wall with your name,
I'd paint it on all the houses,
there wouldn't be a well
I hadn't leaned into
to shout your name there,
nor a stone mountain
where I hadn't uttered
those six separate letters
that are echoed back.

My compulsion is
to teach the birds to sing it,
to teach the fish to drink it,
to teach men that there is nothing
like the madness of repeating your name.

My compulsion is to forget altogether
the other 22 letters, all the numbers,
the books I've read, the poems I've written.
To say hello with your name.
To beg bread with your name.
"She always says the same thing," they'd say when they saw me,
and I'd be so proud, so happy, so self-contained.

And I'll go to the other world with your name on my tongue,
and all their questions I'll answer with your name
—the judges and saints will understand nothing—
God will sentence me to repeating it endlessly and forever.

(Philip Levine
and Ada Long, trs.)

Wild Ballad
For Lucinda, who so loves poetry

Between the stag and the little gazelle
there is no more perfect love.

At dawn they meet beside the lake
and skip a whole day frisking together.

Their love is like the water of the arroyo.
How clear that which brought them together!
The gazelle and the stag walk through
the forest kissing each other in the shadows.

Unselfish love joined them.
The nicest things
in life take place
in the animal world.

A bird sings to a dove,
a lizard waits all night and day...
a beautiful gazelle trembles
because the stag beholds her.

The rock loves the moss,
the wall loves the ivy,
the tree shivers in the wind,
the sea strokes the land.

All of these love freely.
Only man blooms for himself.
The gazelle and the stag stop
in the deepening shadows of the lime trees...

(Philip Levine
and Ada Long, trs.)

I'm Only a Woman

I'm only a woman, and that's enough,
with a goat and an old car,
a "Praise the Lord" every morning,
and a lecherous fool running the show.

I wish I'd been a designer,
or a raving, sensitive Sappho,
look at me
here,
lost
among all these slobs.
I say this for anyone who reads me,
I wanted to be a commander without weapons,
to plant my poems on the moon,
but an astronaut beat me to it.

I wanted to be a pusher of peace on earth—
they arrested me on the road—
I'm only a woman, a full-blooded one,
I'm only a woman, and that's enough.

(Philip Levine
and Ada Long, trs.)

Today Is Sunday

Today is Sunday.
The quiet little afternoon lies beside me.

As always, I am at home,
with three things that have no bodies,
a memory,
a letter,
a photo of my mother.

(Philip Levine
and Ada Long, trs.)

Prayer

Our Father who I know is on earth,
whom I feel in the pine needle,
in the blue shirt of the worker,
in the child bent over her embroidery
winding the thread around a finger.
Our Father who is on earth,
in the furrow,
in the orchard,
in the mine,
in the doorway,
in the movies,
in the wine,
in the doctor's office.
Our Father who is on earth,
where you keep your glory and your hell

and your limbo, which is in the cafes
where the rich drink together.
Our Father who is in the public school,
in the fruit seller,
and in those who go hungry,
and in the poet, but never in the banker.
Our Father who is on earth,
on a park bench in the Prado, reading,
you are the old man who tosses bread to the street birds.
Our Father who is on earth,
in the cigar, in the kiss,
in the ear of corn, in the heart
of all those who are decent.
Father who lives anywhere,
God who penetrates all emptiness,
you who end pain, who is on earth,
our Father whom now we see,
we who will soon see you again
here or in heaven.

(Philip Levine
and Ada Long, trs.)

Painted Windows

I lived in a house
with two real windows and the other two painted on.
Those painted windows caused my first sorrow.
I'd touch the sides of the hall
trying to reach the windows from inside.
I spent my whole childhood wanting
to lean out and see what could be seen

from the windows that weren't there.

(Philip Levine
and Ada Long, trs.)

You'll Get Yours

The dead horse has it all,
the whip is rinsed from his shoulders.

Don't be scared, man,
out of all this nothing lasts.
When that day
of supreme peace arrives
then
there will always be a tree
to offer us four friendly planks;
poor as you are or have been,
in the end you'll have your plot
where you can quietly fall apart.
You'll have your land
and you can command the flowers
brought to the others by their relatives.

(Philip Levine
and Ada Long, trs.)

News

Because sadness pursued me
and I kept meeting it even in my soup,
I've run away to the forest that's off the map,
and even here I'm afraid it will find me.
I'm afraid because I can't forget,
and I'd rather remember nothing.
Because if you want to be happy
you must become an egomaniac
and pluck names from your eyebrows
and run away from the city as I did.

I own nothing but a suit and a diary
and a great fear that my pencil will fail me.

At dawn, only at dawn, I get cold.

The birds and the leaves keep me awake.

Come join me when everything sickens you.
I'm under a roof of leaves
playing a violin with a feather.
If they question you, don't just say anything.
Say, Sadness pursued me
and I looked for freedom on an island
that's off the map.

(Philip Levine
and Ada Long, trs.)

Nikki Giovanni

Nikki Giovanni was born Yolande Cornelia Giovanni, on June 7, 1943, in Knoxville, Tennessee. She entered Fisk University in Nashville but was soon suspended for what school authorities called an inappropriate attitude. Three years later Giovanni returned to Fisk, worked on the campus literary magazine, and graduated with honors in 1967. While at Fisk, she founded a chapter of the Student Non-Violent Coordinating Committee (SNCC). She also attended the University of Pennsylvania School of Social Work and Columbia University's School of the Arts. In 1968 she taught black studies at Queens College and was an associate professor of English at Rutgers University from 1968 to 1972.

Giovanni is a political poet who is deeply committed to furthering the cause of black people. Though the tone of her poetry has softened from an early outspoken militancy, her poems continue to emphasize the importance of the individual and internal change. Her first published book was *Black Feeling, Black Talk* (1968), followed by *Black Judgement* (1969), *Re:Creation* (1970), *Spin a Soft Black Song: Poems for Young People* (1973), *My House* (1972), *The Women and the Men* (1975), *Cotton Candy on a Rainy Day* (1978), *Vacation Time: Poems for Children* (1980), and *Those Who Ride the Night Winds* (1983).

Winter Poem

once a snowflake fell
on my brow and i loved
it so much and i kissed
it and it was happy and called its cousins
and brothers and a web
of snow engulfed me then
i reached to love them all
and i squeezed them and they became
a spring rain and i stood perfectly
still and was a flower

Categories

sometimes you hear a question like "what is
your responsibility as an unwed mother"
and some other times you stand sweating profusely before
going on stage and somebody says "but you are used
    to it"
or maybe you look into a face you've never seen
or never noticed and you know
the ugly awful loneliness of being
locked into a mind and body that belong
to a *name* or *non-name*—not that it matters
cause *you* feel and *it* felt but you have
a planetrainbussubway—it doesn't matter—something
to catch to take your arms away from someone
you might have thought about
putting them around if you didn't
have all that shit to take you safely away

and sometimes on rainy nights you see
an old white woman who maybe you'd really care about
except that you're a young Black woman
whose job it is to kill maim or seriously
make her question
the validity of her existence
and you look at her kind of funny colored eyes
and you think
if she weren't such an aggressive bitch she would see
that if you weren't such a Black one
there would be a relationship but anyway—it doesn't matter
much—except you started out to kill her and now find
you just don't give a damn cause it's all somewhat
    of a bore
so you speak of your mother or sister or very good friend
and really you speak of your feelings which are too
    personal
for anyone else
to take a chance on feeling
and you eat that godawful food and you get somehow
through it and if this seems
like somewhat of a tentative poem it's probably
because i just realized that
i'm bored with categories

Louise Glück

Louise Glück was born in 1943 in New York City. She attended Sarah Lawrence College in 1962 and Columbia University from 1963 to 1965. She has been married twice, presently to John Dranow. They live in Vermont with her son by her first marriage. *Firstborn*, her first poetry collection, appeared in 1968 and was followed by *The House on Marshland* (1975), *The Garden* (1976), *Descending Figure* (1980), and *The Triumph of Achilles* (1985), which won the National Book Critics Circle Award. She has taught poetry writing at Columbia University, the University of Iowa, and Williams College. Glück's poetic vision has won the admiration of critics for its carefully controlled lyricism.

Descending Figure

1   *The Wanderer*

At twilight I went into the street.
The sun hung low in the iron sky,
ringed with cold plumage.
If I could write to you
about this emptiness—
Along the curb, groups of children
were playing in the dry leaves.
Long ago, at this hour, my mother stood
at the lawn's edge, holding my little sister.
Everyone was gone; I was playing
in the dark street with my other sister,

whom death had made so lonely.
Night after night we watched the screened porch
filling with a gold, magnetic light.
Why was she never called?
Often I would let my own name glide past me
though I craved its protection.

2   *The Sick Child*
          —Rijksmuseum

A small child
is ill, has awakened.
It is winter, past midnight
in Antwerp. Above a wooden chest,
the stars shine.
And the child
relaxes in her mother's arms.
The mother does not sleep;
she stares
fixedly into the bright museum.
By spring the child will die.
Then it is wrong, wrong
to hold her—
Let her be alone,
without memory, as the others wake
terrified, scraping the dark
paint from their faces.

3   *For My Sister*

Far away my sister is moving in her crib.
The dead ones are like that,
always the last to quiet.

Because, however long they lie in the earth,
they will not learn to speak
but remain uncertainly pressing against the wooden bars,

so small the leaves hold them down.

Now, if she had a voice,
the cries of hunger would be beginning.
I should go to her;
perhaps if I sang very softly,
her skin so white,
her head covered with black feathers...

The Mirror

Watching you in the mirror I wonder
what it is like to be so beautiful
and why you do not love
but cut yourself, shaving
like a blind man. I think you let me stare
so you can turn against yourself
with greater violence,
needing to show me how you scrape the flesh away
scornfully and without hesitation
until I see you correctly,
as a man bleeding, not
the reflection I desire.

Swans

You were both quiet, looking out over the water.
It was not now; it was years ago,
before you were married.
The sky above the sea had turned
the odd pale peach color of early evening
from which the sea withdrew, bearing
its carved boats: your bodies were like that.
But her face was raised to you,
against the dull waves, simplified
by passion. Then you raised your hand
and from beyond the frame of the dream
swans came to settle on the scaled water.
The sea lay mild as a pool. At its edge,
you faced her, saying
These are yours to keep. The horizon burned,
releasing its withheld light.
And then I woke. But for days
when I tried to imagine you leaving your wife
I saw her motionless before your gift:
always the swans glide unmenacing across
the rigid blue of the Pacific Ocean, then rise
in a single wave, pure white and devouring.

Lamentations

1   *The Logos*

They were both still,
the woman mournful, the man
branching into her body.

But god was watching.
They felt his gold eye
projecting flowers on the landscape.

Who knew what he wanted?
He was god, and a monster.
So they waited. And the world
filled with his radiance,
as though he wanted to be understood.

Far away, in the void that he had shaped,
he turned to his angels.

2   *Nocturne*

A forest rose from the earth.
O pitiful, so needing
God's furious love—

Together they were beasts.
They lay in the fixed
dusk of his negligence;
from the hills, wolves came, mechanically
drawn to their human warmth,
their panic.

Then the angels saw
how He divided them:

the man, the woman, and the woman's body.

Above the churned reeds, the leaves let go
a slow moan of silver.

3   *The Covenant*

Out of fear, they built a dwelling place.
But a child grew between them
as they slept, as they tried
to feed themselves.

They set it on a pile of leaves,
the small discarded body
wrapped in the clean skin
of an animal. Against the black sky
they saw the massive argument of light.

Sometimes it woke. As it reached its hands
they understood they were the mother and father,
there was no authority above them.

4   *The Clearing*

Gradually, over many years,
the fur disappeared from their bodies
until they stood in the bright light
strange to one another.
Nothing was as before.
Their hands trembled, seeking
the familiar.

Nor could they keep their eyes
from the white flesh
on which wounds would show clearly
like words on a page.

And from the meaningless browns and greens
at last God arose, His great shadow
darkening the sleeping bodies of His children,
and leapt into heaven.

How beautiful it must have been,
the earth, that first time
seen from the air.

Anne Hébert

Anne Hébert was born in 1916 in Sainte-Catherine-de-Fossambault, Quebec, Canada. She was educated at home under the close supervision of her father, Maurice Hébert, an official in the provincial government and a noted literary critic. Her father encouraged Hébert to develop her talent for writing stories and sketches; she was also influenced by her cousin, poet Hector de Saint-Denys-Garneau.

Hébert is a respected poet, novelist, and short story writer whose work has frequently anticipated literary developments in the French-language community of Quebec. Much of her work deals with Quebec women trapped in lives of strained, sad domesticity. Her books of poems include *Dreams in Suspension* (1942), *Tomb of the Kings* (1953), and *Poems* (1960); however, she is probably best known for the novel *Kamouraska* (1970), which has been made into a film featuring Genevieve Bujold. Hébert has lived in Paris since 1954.

Our Hands in the Garden

We had this idea
Of planting our hands in the garden

Branches the ten fingers
Little bony trees
Cherished flower-border.

All day we
Waited for the russet bird
And fresh leaves
On our polished nails.

No bird
No springtime
Fell for the snare of our severed hands.

For a single flower
One tiny single star of colour
A single sailing wing
One single note pure white
Given three times

It will take all next season
And our hands melted like water.

(Alan Brown, tr.)

Life in the Castle

It is a castle of forbears
Without fire or table
Dust or tapestry.

The perverse enchantment of the place
Is only in its polished mirrors.

Here there is nothing else to do
But see yourself, day-long, night-long,

Hurl your image at the hard fountain-pools
Your hardest image without shade or colour.

See, how these mirrors are as deep
As cupboards
There's always a dead one living behind the foil
Covering swiftly your reflection
Clinging to you like seaweed

Fitting itself to you, naked and thin,
Simulating love in a slow bitter shudder.

(Alan Brown, tr.)

Landscape

Happed in my rage
As in a mangy coat
I sleep under a rotten bridge
Verdigris and soft lilacs

Dried-out sorrows
Seaweed, oh my lovely dead,
Love changed to salt
And hands lost forever.

On either bank my childhood steams
Sand and marsh insipid memory
Haunted by the raucous cry
Of fancied birds harried by the wind.

(Alan Brown, tr.)

Ping Hsin

Ping Hsin means "ice-heart"; it is the pseudonym of Hsieh Wong-ying. She was born in 1900 in Fukien, China, and grew up near the ocean, on Shantung Peninsula. She lived a tomboy's life, playing near the sea and telling stories to sailors, until she was eleven. In 1911 her family moved back to Fukien, and she began attending missionary schools. She went to Yenching University and studied for her M.A. at Wellesley College in Massachusetts from 1923 to 1926. She spent many years in Japan before returning to the People's Republic of China in 1951, where she became active in various literary organizations until the Cultural Revolution in 1964.

Ping Hsin's first works were not poems but essays and short stories. Even when she began writing the short stanzas of *The Stars* (1921) and *Spring Waters* (1922), she denied it was poetry, referring to it once as "miscellaneous thought." Today she is considered the finest modern Chinese woman poet. She is one of the creators of hsiao-shih: short, compact poems influenced by Japanese haiku.

Remembering

I tear off the calendar,
What day is today?
It is as though a cloud,
Black as a crow,
Swept across my eyes.
I want to be a woman of peace and a philosopher.
I forbid myself to think of him.
But I can think only of him.
I am just the kind of person I am.
I am not a woman of peace.
I am not qualified to be a philosopher.
I only know,
If a man loves me I love him;
If he dislikes me I dislike him.
A piece of land small as a leaf
Will be my home. I can never forget him.

(Kenneth Rexroth
and Ling Chung, trs.)

For the Record
Given to my little brother

His right hand holds his slingshot,
His left a clay pellet.
He sits there, back against a pillar,
His legs straight, watching the sky
With his black eyes,
Stalking the crows that come
To steal the grapes from the arbor.
He intends to kill, but he cannot
Change his expression—filled with affection.
When I suddenly caught sight of him
From the window,
My eyes filled with tears.

(Kenneth Rexroth
and Ling Chung, trs.)

Multitudinous Stars
and Spring Waters, Sel.

I

Sprays of frost flowers form
When the North wind blows gently.

II

Void only—
Take away your veil of stars
Let me worship
The splendor of your face.

III

These fragmented verses
Are only drops of spray
On the sea of knowledge.
Yet they are bright shining
Multitudinous stars, inlaid
On the skies of the heart.

IV

The orphan boat of my heart
Crosses the unsteady, undulant,
Ocean of Time.

V

The commonplace puddle
Reflects the setting sun
And becomes the Sea of Gold.

VI

Oh little island,
How can you be so secure,
When countless great mountains
Have sunk in the sea?

VII

The rose of Heaven—
Its red appears
In contemplative vision.
The pine branch of Heaven—
Its green appears
In contemplative vision.
But the Word of Heaven
Is neither written nor read
In contemplative vision.

VIII

Bright moon—
All grief, sorrow, loneliness completed—
Fields of silver light—
Who, on the other side of the brook
Blows a surging flute?

IX

A trellis of sticks
Crowned with chrysanthemums—
Right there,
You can realize all
The self-sufficient universe.

(Kenneth Rexroth
and Ling Chung, trs.)

Deliverance

Moonlight, clear as water,
I pace the ground under a tree
In deep, deep thought.
Deep in thought, I pick up a fallen twig
To tap, with a sigh, my own shadow
On the moonlit ground.

Life—
Everybody treats it as a dream,
A blurred dream.
My friend,
As you try to find clear lines in the blurred world,
Your life's suffering
Thus begins!

You may treasure life's snow-white robe,
Yet life has to cross
The immense sea of darkness.
My friend,
The world does not abandon you,
Why should you abandon the world?

Let life stand alone and noble like a stork,
Free as a cloud,
And pure and calm as water,
Even if life were a dream,
Let it be a clear dream.

In deep, deep thought—
Deep in thought, I throw away the fallen twig.
Quietly and calmly I gaze at my shadow
On the moonlit ground.

(Kai-yu Hsu, tr.)

The Stars, Sel.

2

Ah, Childhood!
It's the true in a dream,
And a dream among the true,
And the tearful smile in reminiscence.

12

Mankind,
Let us love one another.
We are all travelers on a long journey
Heading for the same destination.

34

The builder of continents
Is not the surging billow
But the tiny grains of sand down beneath.

48

Fragile blades of grass,
Be proud!
Only you so impartially adorn the entire world.

52

The flowers and rocks beside the railroad tracks!
In this instant
You and I
Chance to meet among the infinite beings,
Also bid our last farewell among the infinite beings.
When I return,

In the midst of the myriads of our kind,
Where can I ever find you again?

(Kai-yu Hsu, tr.)

Ingrid Jonker

Ingrid Jonker was born in 1933 on her mother's family's farm near Kimberly, South Africa. Her parents were separated before her birth. As a child, she, her mother, her grandmother, and her sister moved from room to room on the fringes of Cape Town, living in various degrees of poverty. When Jonker was ten years old her mother died, and she was sent to school in Cape Town. Later she was taken in by her father but was treated as an outsider in his house. Abraham Jonker was a member of Parliament and a leading politician in the Nationalist Party.

Jonker began writing poetry as a youngster. Her first book, *Escape,* was published in 1956. Her second book, *Smoke and Ochre* (1963), won a prize, and she used the prize money to travel to Europe. Over the years, Jonker fought with her father over granting political rights to South African blacks and publicly disagreed with him over the censorship laws that he advocated. In 1965 Jonker drowned herself in the sea at Green Point, Cape Town. Her final book of poems, *Setting Sun,* appeared posthumously. Jonker wrote in her native Afrikaans language about deprived and oppressed people and about her own struggle for self-knowledge.

Dark Stream

Green stream full of life
that the sun looks into
with you I cannot talk
you have too many secrets.
Shall I talk with the little tadpoles?
They are too shy.
They say they're going to become big frogs?
It's too uncertain.
Go weep because one sinks
before his back-legs are out?
It's too insignificant.
Stream in which the darkness
sees only the darkness
with you I can speak
I know you better.

(Jack Cope
and William Plomer, trs.)

June Jordan

June Jordan, the daughter of Jamaican immigrants, was born in Harlem, New York City, in 1936. The family moved to the Bedford-Stuyvesant section of Brooklyn when she was five years old. Her father, a post-office clerk, and her mother, a nurse, sent Jordan to Northfield School for Girls, a nearly all-white preparatory school in Massachusetts. Here she was encouraged to write poetry, but she has said that the only models offered to her were white males. Despite this, and her parent's opposition, Jordan decided to become a writer.

In 1953 Jordan entered Barnard College, and in 1955 she met and married Michael Meyer, a white student attending Columbia University. She went with him to the University of Chicago and studied there for one year before returning to Barnard. In 1958 she gave birth to their only son; they were divorced seven years later. During the sixties Jordan was the associate producer of Frederick Wiseman's film about Harlem, *The Cool World,* and was also a researcher and writer for the Technical Housing Department of Mobilization for Youth. She began teaching in 1967 at City College of New York. She is now a tenured professor at the State University of New York at Stony Brook.

Jordan's first book, *Who Look at Me,* appeared in 1969. This work, completed by Jordan, was in fact a project Langston Hughes had begun, just before his death, on the subject of race relations. Two anthologies edited by Jordan came out the following year, *Soulscript* and *The Voice of the Children.* Her first collection of poetry was *Some Changes,* published the same year as her first novel, *His Own Where.* Her second book of poetry, *New Days: Poems of Exile and Return* (1974), was followed by *Things That I Do in the Dark: Selected Poetry* (1977), edited by Toni Morrison,

and *Passion: New Poems, 1977-1980* (1980). Jordan has also written
several books for children. Her collection of essays, *Civil Wars*
(1981), addresses topics such as feminism, the black experience, and
children. Jordan's writing is compelling on many levels as personal
revelation and social awareness infuse her bold style.

Roman Poem Number Two

Toward the end of twenty minutes
we come to a still standing archway
in the city dump
nearby the motorcycle the treetrunk garbage
on the heavy smelling ground

as laurel bay leaves
(grecian laurel) break into

a heavy smell

Nicholas and Florence sharp last night
in life without an urban crisis that be-
longs to you

no demon in the throat of them
but sometimes just a harping on
the silence

No.

"What do you mean, *the subject?* That
has nothing to do with it."

"Listen I teethed on the Brooklyn Bridge"

she will insist her

refugee brown eyes and
hair showing artificial yellow

One can see how color is particularly hard
to manage in a personal way.

"I know every lamppost," she goes on. She does.

Her husband adds another ending
to the movie we
Americans watched in American English
smack in the middle of this wonderful
Italian little Italian slum

"Let's put your money in the bank
—the retarded movie hero—he
would have been smiling at the heroine.
And that would have been," her husband continues
he repeats himself, "That would have been

a wonderful ending."

At this point his wife interrupts his
improvisation.

At the next evening table over espresso

the young woman married to a
well-educated employee
a first-rate worker in the First
National Bank Abroad

exclaims

"I have spent 3 days by myself!

Can you imagine?"

II
On that day exactly when
Christ was born
where the children sprawl and laugh out loud
where the disappearing churchclock only
bells from twelve to two
where I could break my cup of coffee
throwing wakeup at the knowing nuns
where we sit so close we see
each other sideways

the cobblestones turned black
with holy oil

but now ten lire
would be hard to find

and some of us seem
lost

Poem: On Your Love

Beloved
where I have been
if
you loved me more than your own
and God's
soul
you could not have lifted me
out of the water

or
lit even one of the cigarettes I stood
smoking alone.

Beloved
what I have done
if
you discounted the devil
entirely
and rejected the truth as a rumor
you
would turn from the heat of my face
that burns
under your lips.

Beloved
what I have dreamed
if
you ended the fevers and riot
the claw and the wail and the absolute
furious
dishevel of my unkept mind
you
could never believe the quiet
your arms
make true around me.

In your love I am sometimes redeemed
a stranger
to myself.

West Coast Episode

Eddie hung a light globe with the best electric
tape
he could find in
five minutes

then he left the room where he lives

to meet me

        (in Los Angeles)

Meanwhile the light globe fell and
smashed glass everywhere

        (the waterbed
        was dangerous
        for days)

but we used the paper bag that hid
the dollar-twenty-nine-California-Champagne
to hide
the light bulb
with a warm brown atmosphere

and that
worked really well

so there was no problem
except
we had to walk like feet
on broken seashells
even though
the color of the rug was green
and out beyond the one room

of our love
the world was mostly
dry.

Poem: Of Nightsong and Flight

There are things lovely and dangerous still

the rain
when the heat of an evening
sweetens the darkness with mist

and the eyes cannot see what the memory will
of new pain

when the headlights deceive
like the windows wild birds believe to be air
and bash bodies and wings
on the glass

when the headlights show space
but the house and the room and the bed and your face
are still there

while I am mistaken
and try to drive by

the actual kiss
of the world everywhere

Shiraishi Kazuko

Shiraishi Kazuko was born in 1931 in Vancouver, Canada, and did not move to Japan until she was seven. She began publishing poetry as a young girl and developed an energetic personal style that has evoked comparisons to the poetry of Allen Ginsberg, an American poet of the "beat movement." She has written many poetry books, magazine columns, and works of fiction, and she appears on television frequently. Kazuko is considered by some to be Japan's leading contemporary poet.

I Fire at the Face of the Country Where I Was Born

I fire at the face
Of the country where I was born,
At the glazed forehead,
At the sea birds perched,
On that forehead—
Vancouver, beautiful city,
I shoot you because I love you.
Gasoline city, neither one thing nor another.
Neither
A prisoners' ward—without bars,
Nor the loneliness excreted
By lonely youth
I wish it could be
a liberation ward,
a liberation ward, where petals of free thighs

dance in the sky,
a freedom ward,
a happiness ward,
a goddamn it ward,
a goddamn it divine ward,
a profanation ward,
a devil's marriage ward,
a rich diet ward,
a senior citizen's lasciviousness ward,
a wanton woman ward,
a handsome boy ward,
a homosexual ward,
a wanderer's ward,
In the morning of this beautiful city,
With beautiful Lion Head Mountain,
Covered with snow,
In the deep blue sky that soaks
Into the back of my eyes,
I find myself washing my face and teeth
In front of the washing bowl.
It's so sanitary—
A toothbrush and toothpaste kind of purity.
There is not a single bacterium in this
    country.
Not even that little tiny bacterium
Which the Devil called the soul can grow.
It doesn't exist.
All of them,
The King named Old Morality,
The people in power,
Who clothed the honest citizen
And named him Unseen Conservative,
Who stands at the bus stops—
One of them is a platinum blonde girl
Two of them are old women on pensions.
But nobody knows that the story
Of the beautiful girl who sleeps in the forest

Is about Vancouver.
No one knows that this beautiful city
Is the model for that beauty.
Victoria Vancouver, a girl,
A beautiful girl slowly coming towards me
Who opens her eyes but stays asleep
And comes to me smiling
A diplomatic smile.
I aim at the face of this country
Where I was born, and at the seabirds
Perched on the sleepwalker's forehead.
And then,
As the waves splash, moment by moment,
I stand ready to fire
With the pistol of confession.

(Kenneth Rexroth
and Ikuko Atsumi, trs.)

A Chinese Ulysses

Turning back, he found no face,
No newborn face of his own.
Face is a country,
And his country was won away by red
    thoughts.
No longer with a face,
And with no lips to kiss,
He moves on.

His native land is under an unfamiliar map.
Only his mother's womb

Is the sign of a passport from his country of
  birth.
He fumbles for a name.
He left his country.
He is Ulysses
Who knows no return—
Ulysses barred from returning—
Ulysses who has no possible date of
  returning.
Holding wife, children, and flowers,
Burning a torch of poetry,
He cries toward the open sea,
"Is anybody there?"
Any faces proving he really exists?
A thousand, a million, a billion changing
  forms
Make love with the night sea and the stars
  falling on the waves
He enters their music
Seeking his interior country.
He joins the ascetics of love making
Though he can create thousands,
Tens of thousands, of his descendants' faces,
He'll never meet
Nor touch
The face of his newborn country.
So today,
Today again,
Ulysses
Crosses the sea and reaches land.
In a cold country town of Midwest America.
He enters a building
At two in the afternoon.
Nobody
Pays any attention to him.
He is neither a personal attendant to the
  President,

Nor a gangster with a revolver,
Nor a muscle-bound world champion boxer.
He is tall and beautiful with a straight nose,
And he carries a hidden dignity and fire,
But has no other characteristics.
So unless he is violent
Or wears medals of honor
People will just pass him by
Because philosophy is an invisible living
    thing.
Nowadays people aren't scared of ghosts,
Especially living ghosts,
So he goes unnoticed for thousands of years.
He never dies.
He is not allowed to die.
He is Ulysses
A living myth.

"I feel wonderful today!"
He tells me while drunk.
But can he really feel drunk,
Can he get drunk in the sea of liquor
Listening to Sirens?

(Kenneth Rexroth
and Ikuko Atsumi, trs.)

Nagase Kiyoko

Nagase Kiyoko was born in 1906 in Okayama prefecture, Japan.
Her best known poetry collections are *Big Trees* and *Angles of
Various Countries*; she has also written several essays on poetics.
Her poetry often explores the theme of human, especially familial,
relationships.

Mother

I am always aware of my mother,
ominous, threatening,
a pain in the depths of my consciousness.
My mother is like a shell,
so easily broken.
Yet the fact that I was born
bearing my mother's shadow
cannot be changed.
She is like a cherished, bitter dream
my nerves cannot forget
even after I awake.
She prevents all freedom of movement.
If I move she quickly breaks,
and the splinters stab me.

(Kenneth Rexroth
and Ikuko Atsumi, trs.)

Denise Levertov

Denise Levertov was born in 1923. Though considered an American poet, she was born and raised in Ilford, a suburb of London. She was educated at home by her parents, a Welsh mother and a Russian-Jewish father who converted to Christianity and became an Anglican minister. Levertov began writing poetry as a child; when she was twelve she sent some of her poems to T.S. Eliot and received a letter of advice in response. During World War II she worked as a nurse while continuing to write. Her first book of poems, *The Double Image*, appeared in 1946. In 1947 Levertov married American soldier and novelist Mitchell Goodman. She immigrated with him to the United States in 1948 and became a citizen in 1955. The couple has one son, Nikolai, born in 1949. Levertov's second volume of verse, *Here and Now* (1956), appeared ten years after the publication of her first book, and it represents a marked change in style. These poems reflect her deliberate new interest in post-modern poetics and a departure from the nostalgia and abstraction that dominated her earlier work. Some of the many books that followed are: *Overland to the Islands* (1958), The Jacob's Ladder (1961), *O Taste and See* (1964), *The Sorrow Dance* (1967), *Relearning the Alphabet* (1970), *The Freeing of the Dust* (1975), *Candles in Babylon* (1982), and *Breathing Water* (1986).

Levertov has taught at Tufts, Stanford, and other universities, has served as poetry editor of *The Nation*, and is well-known for her work protesting the war in Vietnam. She has translated poems from many languages and has written numerous essays, including several that discuss her theories of poetry. According to the free-verse style that she calls "organic form," words are given to a vision which is necessarily revised through the writing process. This theory of language as experience suggests that poems evolve as they are written and are not wholly preconceived. Her poems aptly demonstrate her poetic ideal: "a sonic, sensuous event."

A Common Ground

i

To stand on common ground
here and there gritty with pebbles
yet elsewhere 'fine and mellow—
uncommon fine for ploughing'

there to labor
planting the vegetable words
diversely in their order
that they come to virtue!

To reach those shining pebbles,
that soil where uncommon men
have labored in their virtue
and left a store

of seeds for planting!
To crunch on words
grown in grit or fine
crumbling earth, sweet

to eat and sweet
to be given, to be eaten
in common, by laborer
and hungry wanderer...

ii

In time of blossoming,
of red
buds, of red
margins upon
white petals among the
new green, of coppery
leaf-buds still weakly
folded, fuzzed
with silver hairs—

when on the grass verges
or elephant-hide rocks, the lunch hour
expands, the girls
laugh at the sun, men
in business suits awkwardly
recline, the petals
float and fall into
crumpled wax-paper, cartons
of hot coffee—

to speak as the sun's
deep tone of May gold speaks
or the spring chill in the rock's shadow,
a piercing minor scale running across the flesh
aslant—or petals
that dream their way
(speaking by being white
by being
curved, green-centered, falling
already while their tree
is half-red with buds) into

human lives! Poems stirred
into paper coffee-cups, eaten
with petals on rye in the

sun—the cold shadows in back,
and the traffic grinding the
borders of spring—entering
human lives forever,
unobserved, a spring element...

iii

*...everything in the world must
excel itself to be itself.*
                   —Pasternak

Not 'common speech'
a dead level
but the uncommon speech of paradise,
tongue in which oracles
speak to beggars and pilgrims:

not illusion but what Whitman called
'the path
between reality and the soul,'
a language
excelling itself to be itself,

speech akin to the light
with which at day's end and day's
renewal, mountains
sing to each other across the cold valleys.

O Taste and See

The world is
not with us enough.
O taste and see

the subway Bible poster said,
meaning **The Lord**, meaning
if anything all that lives
to the imagination's tongue,

grief, mercy, language,
tangerine, weather, to
breathe them, bite,
savor, chew, swallow, transform

into our flesh our
deaths, crossing the street, plum, quince,
living in the orchard and being

hungry, and plucking
the fruit.

The Wings

Something hangs in back of me,
I can't see it, can't move it.

I know it's black,
a hump on my back.

It's heavy. You
can't see it.

What's in it? Don't tell me
you don't know. It's

what you told me about—
black

inimical power, cold
whirling out of it and

around me and
sweeping you flat.

But what if,
like a camel, it's

pure energy I store,
and carry humped and heavy?

Not black, not
that terror, stupidity

of cold rage; or black
only for being pent there?

What if released in air

it became a white

source of light, a fountain
of light? Could all that weight

be the power of flight?
Look inward: see me

with embryo wings, one
feathered in soot, the other

blazing ciliations of ember, pale
flare-pinions. Well—

could I go
on one wing,

the white one?

The Earth Worm

The worm artist
out of soil, by passage
of himself
constructing,
Castles of metaphor!
Delicate
        dungeon turrets!
He throws off
artifacts as he
contracts and expands the
muscle of his being,

ringed in himself,
tilling. He
is homage to
earth, aerates
the ground of his living.

Dwellers at the Hermitage

Grief sinks and sinks
into the old mineshaft
under their house,
how deep, who knows.
When they have need
for it, it's there.

Their joys
refused to share themselves,
fed from the hand
of one alone, browsed
for days in dappled
pathless woods
untamed.

Sorrow
is what one shares,
they say;
and happiness, the wistful gold
of our solitudes, is what
our dearest lovers,
our wingéd friends,
leave with us, in trust.

The Soothsayer

My daughters, the old woman says, the weaver
              of fictions, tapestries
              from which she pulls
              only a single thread each day, pursuing
              the theme at night—
my daughters? Delicate bloom
of polished stone. Their hair
ripples and shines like water, and mine
is dry and crisp as moss in fall.

Trunk, limbs, bark; roots under all of it:
the tree I am, she says, blossoms year after year,
random, euphoric;
the bees are young, who nuzzle their fur
into my many fragile hearts.
My daughters
have yet to bear
their fruit,
they have not imagined
the weight of it.

The Passing Bell

One by one
they fall away—

all whom they really
wanted to keep. People.
Things that were more than things.

The dog, the cat,
the doll with a silk dress,
the red penknife:
those were the first to go.

Then father, mother,
sister, brother,
wife and husband.
Now the child.

The child is grown,
the child is gone,
the child has said,
Don't touch me, don't call me,

your lights have gone out,
I don't love you.
No more.

The distant child
casts a tall shadow:
that's the dark.
And they are small.

The world is brittle,
seamed with cracks,
ready to shatter. Now

the old man steps
into a boat,
rows down the rainy street.
Old woman, she climbs up

into the steeple's eye.
Transmogrified, she's
the clapper of the bell.

The tolling begins.

Eeva-Liisa Manner

Born in 1921, Eeva-Liisa Manner has been one of the most influential voices in the modernist poetry movement of Finland, particularly during the 1950's. Her fourth collection, *This Journey* (1956), established her as a major modern poet. Her work reveals the influence of her interests: music, mythology, and oriental philosophy. Manner lived in Spain for several years and has published a novel, *Victors Beware* (1972), about contemporary life in that country. She is also a playwright and has translated Homer as well as Shakespeare into Finnish.

Into the Silence of the Forest

I am like a foolish elk
who sees her reflection in the water
and thinks that she has drowned.

Or what does she think?
Perhaps she sees another elk there.

But there is not that much difference.
I must become what I am
and not what I think I am
or what I would like to be;
nor, either, that which you are (or the other one);

this becoming of mine is a slow disrobing:
to leave the clothing of my individuality

on the common shore and to swim,   .

always I must swim across, always toward the other shore;
already I once saw my cloak of anonymity
                    climb up a steep precipice
and disappear into the silence of the forest, never returning.

                    (Aili Jarvenpa, tr.)

Assimilation

I will show you a way
that I have travelled

if you come
if you come back some day
searching for me

do you see how everything shifts a little every moment
and becomes less pretentious and more primitive
(like pictures drawn by children
or early forms of life: the soul's alphabet)

you will come to a warm region
it is soft and hazy
but then I will no longer be me,

but the forest.

                    (Aili Jarvenpa, tr.)

From My Life I Make a Poem

From my life I make a poem, from a poem a life,
a poem is a way to live and the only way to die
with ecstatic indifference:
glide into infinity, drift
at God's level for a special weightless moment,
level with God's cold eyes,

that do not weep, do not stay awake, do not form opinions,
watch with disinterest, favoring everything,
pursue order and strictly scheduled moments,
protect scorpions, snakes, cuttle-fish
(which humans hate, confusing these forms
with their own passions);

a poem acknowledges one religion: Curiosity,
wander through the habitats of Pisces, Scorpio and Capricorn,
Borrowing from a bird desire and flight
and floats down
        like a wing wrapped in the wind,
swift freedom, like a bird.

(Aili Jarvenpa, tr.)

Strontium

Scuttle
your world. Imagination has already done it.
The Venus wave circles like a betrothed scorpion round the globe—
just a sufficiently hot embrace,
and love, death resembling the tail feathers,
will destroy the rest.
The spores are floating through the air,
the cloud grows more intense and returns.
The cup of heaven is already full:
                    Nine destructions.
                    Eight terrors.
And the world wanders on
an empty buoy severed from its anchor
deceived, encircled by railroads, exchanged
for dreams whose core was sick,
heavier than lead.
                    No world
could stand a burden of such dreams.
How could a hand which loved flowers
give the world such a gift?

Empty hospitals Empty corridors Empty flues lost echoes
Empty mussels Who had glued his house
Empty leaves Empty glued-on letters
Empty clocks Time has left its home
The hours have moved off
all twelve soundless women
They have covered the windows of heaven and earth
they are watching in silence The houses would weep
if their cleft eyes
had the power to see:

The wires are hanging down over streets and roads,
the words have floated away like rainwater,

rails stick out, a streetcar
full of posters executed on a pole,
a bull pierced with the innocent side open.
Boston has floated off to the Japanese
where Warsaw and Viborg and Vienna
raise their sunset towers
there where my city
raises its peacock color
the streets are changing their patterns
in the streets there are poems like children
born out of the morning, playing with verbs

On the merry meadows
the blue-skirted children are no longer
romping rose-fingered
the confidants of the flowers
On the streets
no red hoops are playing
joy brings no news
the pigeons do not kiss
The trees do not bend
their fragrant burden
the wind cannot remember
purl my well
the shadows of the lovers
are not united
in the alleys of memory and oblivion
no one remembers

A tank has come to a stop in the field
The trench of the buttercup is growing
On the roof of the bunker fog-enveloped grass grows
like a lace to the emptiness

And turned around by the air pressure the radioactive families
stagger, empty bones,
a swollen corpse is swimming in the canal with its feet toward the sea,

the fighter fish has gotten himself a wife for his helmet
and is celebrating his wedding with glittering sides

On the dock lies an exhausted daily paper
with open wings
the ink fading:
Holland ist in Not
Holland gibt's nicht mehr
The corpse has reached its goal
The world has shaken off its illness

The Weltall rises, an enormous bat,
terrible, immeasurable wings,
the armies in its creases, a forest of spears,
fame and honor and religious pestilences.

Welt als Wille und Vorstellung
Die Welt als Wolle die Welt als Hölle und als Verstelltheit
A mammal with a wolf's face A huge squealer
tasted all the diseases collected all odors
spreading itself out
coming to the molten magma

And the stolen planet, disposed of by a lottery
between the great armies as earlier between the gods
divests itself of its beauty for the sake of a blind person.
The playing, dancing, singing animals,
the brilliant fishes and eager birds
are dying.

Barren waste. It is snowing on the mountains. The reeds do not
remember.

On the other side the stars are turning round.

(Martin Allwood, tr.)

At the Street Corner

At the street corner they are already roasting chestnuts on a grill
if you buy a handful you can also warm up.

A hot chestnut, as if one were eating bread,
it serves as bread to many in this place.
The rattle of the wheels, the cries of the vendors,
the sharp, melodic urging of the donkey driver
as he moves the straw, old bits of sunshine
shaking from the straws along the road a brittle music.

The alley elm trees are brown, the reeds burned,
leaves fall, November news.
It is autumn. A sigh through the forest
from tree to tree; the tenderest are already stripping down.

(Martin Allwood, tr.)

The Trees Are Naked

The trees are naked.
Autumn
drives its misty horses to the river.

The dogs are barking far, far away.
Small carts leave the narrow gate
alone, without drivers, and disappear.

One says, That's how a ghost drives,
if the heart is sleeping under a holly tree.
But the ghosts are just memories.

Night comes early.
Soon it will be winter
deep and cold, like a well.

(Martin Allwood, tr.)

The Women Thought Christ Risen

The women thought Christ risen
was a gardener.
There probably lingered round him the scent of flowers and
   fading leaves.
On his way to the earthen village he also appeared to others,
one said: It was he,
another: No, it was a gardener,

and the disciple prayed: "Stay with us,
evening comes fast, and the day is departing."
And he stayed and dined with him and they knew him.

But the gardener returned to the garden
and turned into a tree,
and the tree is no more, only a warm glow,
a very old, very tired glow.

(Martin Allwood, tr.)

Jenny Mastoraki

Jenny Mastoraki is one of the most distinctive contemporary Greek poets. She was born in Athens in 1949 and attended university there, majoring in Byzantine Studies. Her first volume of poetry was *Rights of Way* (1972).

Then They Paraded Pompey's Urn

Then they paraded Pompey's urn
simply and soberly
on the backs of royal elephants.
They lifted it aboard with pulleys
in the port of Haifa,
and the stevedores still brag
how they debauched with him
down by the wharfs.

(Nikos Germanakos, tr.)

The Wooden Horse Then Said

The Wooden Horse then said
no I refuse to see the press
and they said why not and he said
he knew nothing about the killing,
and anyway he himself always ate
lightly in the evenings
and once in his younger days
he'd worked as a pony on a merry-go-round.

(Nikos Germanakos, tr.)

The Crusaders

The Crusaders
knew the Holy Places
only from postcards and tourist guides.
So, they set off
with banners, tents,
tools and sandwiches,
just like a school excursion.
One day, Baldwin's mistress
received a Polaroid snapshot
of some monument or other.
Her beau was marked with an arrow,
one among a dozen heads.
They brought it off—though it was a fluke,
to tell the truth.

The papers of the period

spoke of bloodless operations.

(Nikos Germanakos, tr.)

Cecília Meireles

Cecília Meireles was born in 1901 in Rio de Janeiro, Brazil. Her parents died when she was three, and she was raised by her maternal grandmother. She began writing poetry at the age of nine and became a public schoolteacher when she was sixteen.

Her first published book of poems, *Specters* (1919), established her literary reputation. For years after, she published no more poetry but worked as a journalist, a professor of comparative literature and Oriental languages, and a librarian. She founded the first library of children's literature in Brazil. In 1939, she published *Journey* and continued to publish poetry regularly until her death in 1964. She also wrote plays, translated works into Portuguese, and was an expert in Brazilian folklore.

Meireles' poems are personal and lyrical. Simple in style, they contain complex imagery within traditional forms. She was nominated twice for the Nobel Prize and is regarded as one of Brazil's greatest poets.

The Roosters Will Crow

The roosters will crow when we die,
And a soft breeze, with delicate hands,
Will touch the fringes, the silken
Shrouds.

And the sleep of night will cloud
The clear windows.

And the crickets, far off, will saw silences:
Stalks of crystal, cold long solitudes,
And the enormous perfume of trees.

Ah, what sweet moon will look upon our calm face,
Even yet more calm than her great mirror
Of silver.

What thick freshness upon our hair,
As free as the fields at sunrise.

From the mist of dawn,
One last star
Will ascend: pale.

What immense peace, without human voice,
Without the lip of wolfish faces,
Without hatred, without love, without anything!

Like dark lost prophets,
Only the dogs will talk through the valleys.
Strong questions. Vast pauses.

We shall lie in death
In that soft contour
Of a shell in the water.

                        (John Nist
                        with Yolanda Leite, trs.)

Second Rose Motif
To Mário de Andrade

However much I praise, you do not listen,
although in form and mother-of-pearl you could be
the uttering shell, the ear whose music lesson
engraves the inmost spirals of the sea.

I place you in crystal, in the mirror's prison
past all undertone of well or grotto...
Pure absence, blind incomprehension
offered to the wasp and to the bee

as to your acolyte, O deaf and mute
and blind and beautiful and interminable rose
who into time, attar and verse transmute

yourself now beyond earth or star arisen
to glisten from my dream, of your own beauty
insensible because you do not listen...

                        (James Merrill, tr.)

Vigil

As the companion is dead,
so we must all together die
somewhat.

Shed for him who lost his life,
our tears are worth
nothing.

Love for him, within this grief,
is a faint sigh lost in a vast
forest.

Faith in him, the lost
companion—what but that
is left?

To die ourselves somewhat
through him we see today
quite dead.

                    (James Merrill, tr.)

Ballad of the Ten Casino Dancers

Ten dancers glide
across a mirror floor.
They have thin gilt plaques on Egyptian bodies,
fingertips reddened, blue lids painted,
lift white veils naively scented,
bend yellow knees.

The ten dancers go
voiceless among customers,
hands above knives, teeth above roses,
little lamps befuddled by cigars.
Between the music and the movement flows
depravity, a flight of silken stairs.

The dancers now advance
like ten lost grasshoppers,
advance, recoil, avoiding glances
in the close room, and plucking at the din.
They are so naked, you imagine
them clothed in the stuff of tears.

The ten dancers screen
their pupils under great green lashes.
Death passes tranquil as a belt around
their phosphorescent waists.
As who should bear a dead child to the ground
each bears her flesh that moves and scintillates.

Fat men watch in massive tedium
those cold, cold dancers,
pitiful serpents without appetite
who are children by daylight.
Ten anemic angels made of hollows,
melancholy embalms them.

Ten mummies in a band,
back and forth go the tired dancers.
Branch whose fragrant blossoms bend
blue, green, gold, white.
Ten mothers would weep at the sight
of those dancers hand in hand.

(James Merrill, tr.)

Pyrargyrite Metal, 9

The piano tuner spoke to me, that tenderest
attender to each note
who looking over sharp and flat
hears and glimpses something more remote.
And his ears make no mistake
nor do his hands that in each chord awake
those sounds delighted to keep house together.

"Disinterested is my interest:
I don't confuse music and instrument, mere
piano tuner that I am,
calligrapher of that superhuman speech
which lifts me as a guest to its high sphere.
Oh! what new Physics waits up there to teach
other matters to another ear. . ."

(James Merrill, tr.)

Edna St. Vincent Millay

Edna St. Vincent Millay was born in 1892 and grew up in Camden, Maine. As a child, Millay's musical talent was encouraged by her mother, but her literary interests predominated. Her first published poem, "Forest Trees," appeared in a children's magazine when she was fourteen. When she was twenty, she entered her poem, "Renascence," in an annual contest held by *The Lyric Year* anthology and received immediate critical recognition. In 1914, Millay attended Vassar College on a scholarship and studied literature, drama, and classical and modern languages. Just after her graduation in 1917, her first volume of poetry, *Renascence and Other Poems*, was released.

Out of school, Millay moved to Greenwich Village. There she became part of the comparatively free and open bohemian life that she came to symbolize for other young women. Millay continued to write poetry in New York: *A Few Figs from Thistles* appeared in 1920, followed by *Second April* in 1921. During these years she also acted with the Provincetown Players and wrote such works for the company as the antiwar verse play *Aria da Capo* (1920). In 1923 *The Ballad of the Harp-Weaver* won the Pulitzer Prize for Poetry. Also during that year Millay married Eugen Boissevain, a Dutch importer and widower of feminist Inez Milholland. Their marriage lasted until his death in 1949.

Millay became politically involved during the late twenties and thirties. She was arrested while protesting the trial of Sacco and Vanzetti and wrote a poem condemning their execution. She continued to produce poetry in such volumes as *The Buck in the Snow* (1928), *Fatal Interview* (1931), *Wine from These Grapes* (1934), and *Huntsman, What Quarry?* (1939). She also produced a book of poems, *Make Bright the Arrows* (1940), and a play, *The*

Murder of Lidice (1942), which voiced her alarm at the rise of fascism in Europe.

Though Millay's popularity has dimmed since the 1920's, she remains a major American poet. Unlike other poets of her time, Millay continued to write in the traditional forms of the sonnet, ballad, and lyric. Indeed, her best work uses these rigid forms to balance the intense emotions she expresses on the themes of love, loss, death, and nature. Millay died in 1950.

Spring

To what purpose, April, do you return again?
Beauty is not enough.
You can no longer quiet me with the redness
Of little leaves opening stickily.
I know what I know.
The sun is hot on my neck as I observe
The spikes of the crocus.
The smell of the earth is good.
It is apparent that there is no death.
But what does that signify?
Not only under ground are the brains of men
Eaten by maggots,
Life in itself
Is nothing,
An empty cup, a flight of uncarpeted stairs.
It is not enough that yearly, down this hill,
April
Comes like an idiot, babbling and strewing flowers.

The Bean-Stalk

Ho, Giant! This is I!
I have built me a bean-stalk into your sky!
La,—but it's lovely, up so high!

This is how I came,—I put
Here my knee, there my foot,
Up and up, from shoot to shoot—
And the blessèd bean-stalk thinning
Like the mischief all the time,
Till it took me rocking, spinning,
In a dizzy, sunny circle,
Making angles with the root,
Far and out above the cackle
Of the city I was born in,
Till the little dirty city
In the light so sheer and sunny
Shone as dazzling bright and pretty
As the money that you find
In a dream of finding money—
What a wind! What a morning!—

Till the tiny, shiny city,
When I shot a glance below,
Shaken with a giddy laughter,
Sick and blissfully afraid,
Was a dew-drop on a blade,
And a pair of moments after
Was the whirling guess I made,—
And the wind was like a whip
Cracking past my icy ears,
And my hair stood out behind,
And my eyes were full of tears,
Wide-open and cold,
More tears than they could hold,

The wind was blowing so,
And my teeth were in a row,
Dry and grinning,
And I felt my foot slip,
And I scratched the wind and whined,
And I clutched the stalk and jabbered,
With my eyes shut blind,—
What a wind! What a wind!

Your broad sky, Giant,
Is the shelf of a cupboard;
I make bean-stalks, I'm
A builder, like yourself,
But bean-stalks is my trade,
I couldn't make a shelf,
Don't know how they're made,
Now, a bean-stalk is more pliant—
La, what a climb!

English Sparrows
Washington Square

How sweet the sound in the city an hour before sunrise,
When the park is empty and grey and the light clear and so lovely
I must sit on the floor before my open window for an hour with
    my arms on the sill
And my cheek on my arm, watching the spring sky's
Soft suffusion from the roofed horizon upward with palest rose,
Doting on the charming sight with eyes
Open, eyes closed;
Breathing with quiet pleasure the cool air cleansed by the night,
    lacking all will

To let such happiness go, nor thinking the least thing ill
In me for such indulgence, pleased with the day and with myself.
  How sweet
The noisy chirping of the urchin sparrows from crevice and shelf
Under my window, and from down there in the street,
Announcing the advance of the roaring competitive day with city
  bird-song.

A bumbling bus
Goes under the arch. A man bareheaded and alone
Walks to a bench and sits down.
He breathes the morning with me; his thoughts are his own.
Together we watch the first magnanimous
Rays of the sun on the tops of greening trees and on houses of
  red brick and of stone.

The Rabbit

Hearing the hawk squeal in the high sky
I and the rabbit trembled.
Only the dark small rabbits newly kittled in their neatly dis-
  sembled
Hollowed nest in the thicket thatched with straw
Did not respect his cry.
At least, not that I saw.

But I have said to the rabbit with rage and a hundred times,
  "Hop!
Streak it for the bushes! Why do you sit so still?
You are bigger than a house, I tell you, you are bigger than a
  hill, you are a beacon for air-planes!
O indiscreet!
And the hawk and all my friends are out to kill!

Get under cover!" But the rabbit never stirred; she never will.

And I shall see again and again the large eye blaze
With death, and gently glaze;
The leap into the air I shall see again and again, and the kicking
   feet;
And the sudden quiet everlasting, and the blade of grass green in
   the strange mouth of the interrupted grazer.

Kadia Molodowsky

Kadia Molodowsky was born in Lithuania in 1893 and received her early education from her father. She later became active in the progressive Yiddish education movement in Warsaw during the twenties and thirties, while teaching at Yiddish schools and writing Yiddish verse. Fleeing from Fascist persecution, she immigrated to New York City in 1935. She settled there, making frequent trips to Israel.

Molodowsky became one of the most respected poets in the Yiddish language; she also worked as editor of the Yiddish literary magazine *Sevive*. Her works include the poetry collections *Angels Come to Jerusalem* (1952) and *Light of a Thorn Tree* (1965), the book of children's stories and poems *Marzipans* (1970), the play *Toward the God of the Desert* (1949), and the novel *At the Gate* (1967). Selected English translations of her poems appear in the collection *Onions and Cucumbers and Plums* (1958) by F.Z. Betsky. Molodowsky died in 1975.

Women Songs

I

The faces of women long dead, of our family,
come back in the night, come in dreams to me saying:
We have kept our blood pure through long generations,
we brought it to you like a sacred wine
from the kosher cellars of our hearts.
And one of them whispers:
I remained deserted, when my two rosy apples
still hung on the tree
and I gritted away the long nights of waking between my white
    teeth.

I will go meet the grandmothers, saying:
Your sighs were the whips that lashed me
and drove my young life to the threshold
to escape from your kosher beds.
But wherever the street grows dark you pursue me—
wherever a shadow falls.

Your whimperings race like the autumn wind past me,
and your words are the silken cord
still binding my thoughts,
My life is a page ripped out of a holy book
and part of the first line is missing.

II

There are such spring-like nights here,
when a blade of grass pushes up through the soil
and the fresh dawn is a green pillow
under the skeleton of a dead horse.
And all the limbs of a woman plead for the ache of birth.
And women come down to lie like sick sheep

by the wells—to heal their bodies,
their faces blackened with year-long thirst for a child's cry.

There are such spring-like nights here
when lightning pierces the black soil with silver knives
and pregnant women approach the white tables of the hospital
with quiet steps
and smile at the unborn child
and perhaps at death.

There are such spring-like nights here
when a blade of grass pushes up through the soil.

(Adrienne Rich, tr.)

Song of the Sabbath

I quarreled with kings till the Sabbath,
I fought with the six kings
of the six days of the week.

Sunday they took away my sleep.
Monday they scattered my salt.
And on the third day, my God,
they threw out my bread: whips flashed
across my face. The fourth day
they caught my dove, my flying dove,
and slaughtered it.
It was like that till Friday morning.

This is my whole week,
the dove's flight dying.

At nightfall Friday
I lit four candles,
and the queen of the Sabbath came to me.
Her face lit up the whole world,
and made it all a Sabbath.
My scattered salt
shone in its little bowl,
and my dove, my flying dove,
clapped its wings together,
and licked its throat.
The Sabbath queen blessed my candles,
and they burned with a pure, clean flame.
The light put out the days of the week
and my quarreling with the six kings.

The greenness of the mountains
is the greenness of the Sabbath.
The silver of the lake
is the silver of the Sabbath.
The singing of the wind
is the singing of the Sabbath.

And my heart's song
is an eternal Sabbath.

(Jean Valentine, tr.)

And What Will Happen

And what will happen
when the fliers come back
and say there is no heaven?

Where will I look then,
if not to the sky?

How will I bear the gray rain,
the dust of these stone streets?
How will I keep from turning my heart away?
And who will help with my poems,
if there's no one at all in the sky?

But I won't believe the fliers.
I won't believe them.

For I have seen an angel,
more than once,
and more than once he has saved me
from plagues that threatened.

I will not trust the fliers.
I will not trust them.

And what will happen if the fliers come back
and say there is no paradise,
home of the saints?

How will I walk across papery bridges
if we have no more saints?
How will I fly across chasms and ditches
if I can't hang on to their tails?
Who will keep my hungry soul?
Soothe my crying?

But I will not listen to the fliers.
I won't listen.

For I have seen the saints,
more than once.
They went in yoke and torment,
and carried the world on their backs.

So I will not look at the fliers.
Not notice them.

Heaven can be reached
by those who weave with its blue,
walk on miracles as on stairs,
and know the ways of the secret.

(Jean Valentine, tr.)

White Night

White night, my painful joy,
your light is brighter than the dawn.
A white ship is sailing from East Broadway
where I see no sail by day.

A quiet star hands me a ticket
open for all the seas.
I put on my time-worn jacket
and entrust myself to the night.

Where are you taking me, ship?
Who charted us on this course?

The hieroglyphs of the map escape me,
and the arrows of your compass.

I am the one who sees and does not see.
I go along on your deck of secrets,
squeeze shut my baggage on the wreath of sorrows
from all my plucked-out homes.

—Pack in all my blackened pots,
their split lids, the chipped crockeries,
pack in my chaos with its gold-encrusted buttons
since chaos will always be in fashion.

—Pack the letters stamped *Unknown at This Address*—
vanished addresses that sear my eyes,
postmarked with more than years and days;
sucked into my bones and marrow.

—Pack up my shadow that weighs more than my body,
that comes along with its endless exhortations.
Weekdays or holidays, time of flowers or withering,
my shadow is with me, muttering its troubles.

Find me a place of honey cakes and sweetness
where angels and children picnic together
(this is the dream I love best of all),
Where the sacred wine fizzes in bottles.

Let me have one sip, here on East Broadway,
for the sake of those old Jews crying in the dark.
I cry my heretic's tears with them,
their sobbing is my sobbing.

I'm a difficult passenger, my ship
is packed with the heavy horns, the *shofars* of grief.
Tighten the sails of night as far as you can,
for the daylight cannot carry me.

Take me somewhere to a place of rest,
of goats in belled hats playing on trombones—
to the Almighty's fresh white sheets
where the hunter's shadow cannot fall.

Take me...Yes, take me...But you know best
where the sea calmly opens its blue road.
I'm wearier than your oldest tower;
somewhere I've left my heart aside.

                              (Adrienne Rich, tr.)

God of Mercy

O God of Mercy
For the time being
Choose another people.
We are tired of death, tired of corpses,
We have no more prayers,
For the time being
Choose another people.
We have run out of blood
For victims,
Our houses have been turned into desert,
The earth lacks space for tombstones,
There are no more lamentations
Nor songs of woe
In the ancient texts.

God of Mercy
Sanctify another land
Another Sinai.

We have covered every field and stone
With ashes and holiness.
With our crones
With our young
With our infants
We have paid for each letter in your Commandments.

God of Mercy
Lift up your fiery brow,
Look on the peoples of the world,
Let them have the prophecies and Holy Days
Who mumble your words in every tongue.
Teach them the Deeds
And the ways of temptation.

God of Mercy
To us give rough clothing
Of shepherds who tend sheep
Of blacksmiths at the hammer
Of washerwomen, cattle slaughterers
And lower still.
And O God of Mercy
Grant us one more blessing—
Take back the gift of our separateness.

(Irving Howe, tr.)

Marianne Moore

Marianne Moore was born in Kirkwood, Missouri, in 1887. Her father, John Milton Moore, an engineer and inventor, suffered a nervous breakdown and was institutionalized just before Moore was born. She was raised by her mother, Mary Warner Moore, and her grandfather, a Presbyterian minister. When Moore was seven her grandfather died and she, her mother, and brother moved to Carlisle, Pennsylvania. Her mother taught English at Metzger Institute, and Moore attended preparatory school there. She went on to Bryn Mawr College, where she studied biology and histology and contributed to the campus literary magazine. She received a B.A. in 1909. After graduation, Moore took business courses at Carlisle Commercial College. Then, from 1911 to 1915, she taught secretarial skills and commercial law while coaching boys' field sports at the United States Industrial Indian School in Carlisle.

Moore continued to write, and in April 1915 two of her poems appeared in *The Egoist*, a London literary magazine. Soon her work appeared in *Poetry* and *Others*, a New York magazine. Meanwhile, Marianne and her mother moved to New Jersey to be with her brother, Warner, now a Presbyterian minister. When he joined the Navy during World War I, they moved to Greenwich Village where Moore worked as a secretary and tutor at a girls' school and then at the New York Public Library.

During these years, Moore became friends with such leading literary figures as William Carlos Williams, E.E. Cummings, Hart Crane, and critic Arthur Kreymbourg. She continued to publish poems in journals and magazines, and in 1921 her first collection, *Poems*, appeared in London. This volume was brought out without Moore's knowledge by her friends, H.D. and Winifred Ellerman ("Bryher"). Moore herself oversaw the publication of *Observations* (1924), which won the Dial Award. From 1925 to 1929 she was the editor of *The Dial*, a prestigious New York literary magazine. In 1935 *Selected Poems* appeared, with an introduction by T.S. Eliot. Moore, who revised poems throughout her career, continued to produce books of new, old, and reworked poems, including *The Pangolin and Other Verse* (1936), *What Are Years* (1941), *Nevertheless* (1944), *Collected Poems* (1951), *O To Be a Dragon* (1959), and *Selected Poems* (1969). *The Complete Poems of Marianne Moore* appeared in 1981. She also translated the fables of La Fontaine (1954) and wrote a book of critical essays, *Predilections* (1955), on Louise Bogan, Ezra Pound, Anna Pavlova, and others.

Though she never became a widely-read poet, Moore's work was hailed critically. *Collected Poems* (1951) won the National Book Award, the Pulitzer Prize, and the Bollingen Prize in Poetry. By 1955 when she was elected to the American Academy of Arts and Letters, her literary reputation was known by many who had never read her poems.

Moore's poetry has been appreciated the most by her fellow poets, who admire the craftsmanship of her distinctively structured stanzas, the careful choice of words, and the intellectually inventive imagery. She frequently draws on the observation of animals, works of art, and everyday events such as baseball games to create analogies that often contain a moral. Moore died in 1972.

To a Prize Bird

You suit me well; for you can make me laugh,
nor are you blinded by the chaff
    that every wind sends spinning from the rick.

You know to think, and what you think you speak
with much of Samson's pride and bleak
    finality; and none dare bid you stop.

Pride sits you well, so strut, colossal bird.
No barnyard makes you look absurd;
    your brazen claws are staunch against defeat.

To Statecraft Embalmed

There is nothing to be said for you. Guard
your secret. Conceal it under your hard
    plumage, necromancer.
        O
bird, whose tents were "awnings of Egyptian
yarn," shall Justice' faint zigzag inscription—
    leaning like a dancer—
        show
the pulse of its once vivid sovereignty?
You say not, and transmigrating from the
    sarcophagus, you wind
        snow
silence round us and with moribund talk,
half limping and half ladyfied, you stalk
    about. Ibis, we find

no
virtue in you—alive and yet so dumb.
Discreet behavior is not now the sum
    of statesmanlike good sense.
    Though
it were the incarnation of dead grace?
As if a death mask ever could replace
    life's faulty excellence!
    Slow
to remark the steep, too strict proportion
of your throne, you'll see the wrenched distortion
    of suicidal dreams
        go
staggering toward itself and with its bill
attack its own identity, until
    foe seems friend and friend seems
        foe.

Those Various Scalpels,

those
various sounds consistently indistinct, like intermingled echoes
    struck from thin glasses successively at random—
        the inflection disguised: your hair, the tails of two
    fighting-cocks head to head in stone like sculptured scimitars re-
        peating the curve of your ears in reverse order: your eyes,
                                flowers of ice and snow

sown by tearing winds on the cordage of disabled ships; your
                                raised hand,
    an ambiguous signature: your cheeks, those rosettes
        of blood on the stone floors of French châteaux,

with regard to which the guides are so affirmative—your other
hand,

a bundle of lances all alike, partly hid by emeralds from Persia
and the fractional magnificence of Florentine
goldwork—a collection of little objects—
sapphires set with emeralds, and pearls with a moonstone,
made fine
with enamel in gray, yellow, and dragonfly blue; a lemon,
a pear

and three bunches of grapes, tied with silver: your dress, a
magnificent square
cathedral tower of uniform
and at the same time diverse appearance—a
species of vertical vineyard rustling in the storm
of conventional opinion. Are they weapons or scalpels?
Whetted to brilliance

by the hard majesty of that sophistication which is superior to
opportunity,
these things are rich instruments with which to experiment.
But why dissect destiny with instruments
more highly specialized than components of destiny itself?

To a Steam Roller

The illustration
is nothing to you without the application.
    You lack half wit. You crush all the particles down
        into close conformity, and then walk back and forth on them.

Sparkling chips of rock
are crushed down to the level of the parent block.
    Were not "impersonal judgment in aesthetic
        matters, a metaphysical impossibility," you

might fairly achieve
it. As for butterflies, I can hardly conceive
    of one's attending upon you, but to question
        the congruence of the complement is vain, if it exists.

Sojourn in the Whale

Trying to open locked doors with a sword, threading
    the points of needles, planting shade trees
    upside down; swallowed by the opaqueness of one whom the

                                                            seas

love better than they love you, Ireland—

you have lived and lived on every kind of shortage.
    You have been compelled by hags to spin
    gold thread from straw and have heard men say:
"There is a feminine temperament in direct contrast to ours

which makes her do these things. Circumscribed by a
    heritage of blindness and native
    incompetence, she will become wise and will be forced to give in.
Compelled by experience, she will turn back;

water seeks its own level":
    and you have smiled. "Water in motion is far
    from level." You have seen it, when obstacles happened to bar
the path, rise automatically.

Nevertheless

you've seen a strawberry
    that's had a struggle; yet
    was, where the fragments met,

a hedgehog or a star-
    fish for the multitude
    of seeds. What better food

than apple seeds—the fruit
    within the fruit—locked in
    like counter-curved twin

hazelnuts? Frost that kills
    the little rubber-plant-
    leaves of *kok-saghyz*-stalks, can't

harm the roots; they still grow
    in frozen ground. Once where
    there was a prickly-pear-

leaf clinging to barbed wire,
    a root shot down to grow
    in earth two feet below;

as carrots form mandrakes
    or a ram's-horn root some-
    times. Victory won't come

to me unless I go
    to it; a grape tendril
    ties a knot in knots till

Eiléan Ní Chuilleanáin

Eiléan Ní Chuilleanáin was born in 1942 in Cork, Ireland, and was educated at University College, Cork, and at Oxford, England. Since 1966 she has been a lecturer in Renaissance English at Trinity College, Dublin, and has served as co-editor of *Cyphers*, a Dublin literary magazine. Ní Chuilleanáin is one of the most respected contemporary Irish poets. The style and tone of her work reflect her interest in history, mythology, and the haunting beauty of the Irish countryside. Her poetry publications include *Acts and Monuments* (1972), *Site of Ambush* (1975), which received the Irish Publishers Award in 1976, *The Second Voyage* (1977), and *The Rose Geranium* (1981).

Swineherd

"When all this is over," said the swineherd,
"I mean to retire, where
Nobody will have heard about my special skills
And conversation is mainly about the weather.

I intend to learn how to make coffee at least as well
As the Portuguese lay-sister in the kitchen
And polish the brass fenders every day.
I want to lie awake at night
Listening to cream crawling to the top of the jug
And the water lying soft in the cistern.

I want to see an orchard where the trees grow in straight

lines
And the yellow fox finds shelter between the navy-blue
   trunks,
Where it gets dark early in summer
And the apple-blossom is allowed to wither on the bough."

Dead Fly

Sparafucile fought his peasant war
Although his grey crudely-slung chassis lacked
The jet lines of midge or mosquito,
The wasp's armour, the spider's intellectual speed;
Still the rough guerilla survived my stalking,
Until by mistake I closed a bible
And cramped his limbs to soak in his scarce blood.

A monk that read this book and lived alone
Domesticated an insect of your kind,
Taught him to stand and mark the words on the page
And live in peace inside the same stone house
With a mouse he kept to bite his ear
Whenever he winked, and a cock that blasted him
Out of his bed for matins in the dark.

Planting these three companions as watchmen
At the frontiers of his ambition, he forgot
Mortality, till death knocked them off in a row.
He complained to his friend the exile, across the profound
Indelible sea. Roused by the frosty wind
Of a friend's voice, the thought of home stinging
Fresh and sweet as the smell of oranges,

He considered the island, so far away now it shone
Bright as a theory or a stained-glass window,
Coloured and clear in the sun, his austere mind
Half sure he had invented it, and replied:
To possess is to be capable of loss
Which no possible profit can reconcile
As David, his kingdom sure, could not forget Saul.

Lucina Schynning in Silence of the Night...

Moon shining in silence of the night
The heaven being all full of stars
I was reading my book in a ruin
By a sour candle, without roast meat or music
Strong drink or a shield from the air
Blowing in the crazed window, and I felt
Moonlight on my head, clear after three days' rain.

I washed in cold water; it was orange, channelled down
     bogs
Dipped between cresses.
The bats flew through my room where I slept safely;
Sheep stared at me when I woke.

Behind me the waves of darkness lay, the plague
Of mice, plague of beetles
Crawling out of the spines of books,
Plague shadowing pale faces with clay
The disease of the moon gone astray.

In the desert I relaxed, amazed
As the mosaic beasts on the chapel floor

When Cromwell had departed and they saw
The sky growing through the hole in the roof.

Sheepdogs embraced me; the grasshopper
Returned with a lark and bee.
I looked down between hedges of high thorn and saw
The hare, absorbed, sitting still
In the middle of the track; I heard
Again the chirp of the stream running.

Old Roads

Missing from the map, the abandoned roads
Reach across the mountain, threading into
Clefts and valleys, shuffle between thick
Hedges of flowery thorn.
The grass flows into tracks of wheels,
Mowed evenly by the careful sheep;
Drenched, it guards the gaps of silence
Only trampled on the pattern day.

And if, an odd time, late
At night, a cart passes
Splashing in a burst stream, crunching bones,
The wavering candle hung by the shaft
Slaps light against a single gable
Catches a flat tombstone
Shaking a nervous beam in a white face

Their arthritic fingers
Their stiffening grasp cannot
Hold long on the hillside—

Slowly the old roads lose their grip.

Early Recollections

If I produce paralysis in verse
Where anger would be more suitable,
Could it be because my education
Left out the sight of death?
They never waked my aunt Nora in the front parlour;
Our cats hunted mice but never
Showed us what they killed.
I was born in the war but never noticed.
My aunt Nora is still in the best of health
And her best china has not been changed or broken.
Dust has not settled on it; I noticed it first
The same year that I saw
How the colours of stones change as water
Dries off them after rain.
I know how things begin to happen
But never expect an end.

Dearest,
       if I can never write 'goodbye'
On the torn final sheet, do not
Investigate my adult life but try
Where I started. My
Childhood gave me hope
And no warnings.
I discovered the habits of moss
That secretly freezes the stone,
Rust softly biting the hinges
To keep the door always open.
I became aware of truth
Like the tide helplessly rising and falling in one place.

The Second Voyage

Odysseus rested on his oar and saw
The ruffled foreheads of the waves
Crocodiling and mincing past: he rammed
The oar between their jaws and looked down
In the simmering sea where scribbles of weed defined
Uncertain depth, and the slim fishes progressed
In fatal formation, and thought
                If there was a single
Streak of decency in these waves now, they'd be ridged
Pocked and dented with the battering they've had,
And we could name them as Adam named the beasts,
Saluting a new one with dismay, or a notorious one
With admiration; they'd notice us passing
And rejoice at our shipwreck, but these
Have less character than sheep and need more patience.

I know what I'll do he said;
I'll park my ship in the crook of a long pier
(And I'll take you with me he said to the oar)
I'll face the rising ground and walk away
From tidal waters, up riverbeds
Where herons parcel out the miles of stream,
Over gaps in the hills, through warm
Silent valleys, and when I meet a farmer
Bold enough to look me in the eye
With 'where are you off to with that long
Winnowing fan over your shoulder?'
There I will stand still
And I'll plant you for a gatepost or a hitching-post
And leave you as a tidemark. I can go back
And organize my house then.
                           But the profound
Unfenced valleys of the ocean still held him;
He had only the oar to make them keep their distance;
The sea was still frying under the ship's side.
He considered the water-lilies, and thought about fountains
Spraying as wide as willows in empty squares,
The sugarstick of water clattering into the kettle,
The flat lakes bisecting the rushes. He remembered spiders and frogs
Housekeeping at the roadside in brown trickles floored with mud,
Horsetroughs, the black canal, pale swans at dark.
His face grew damp with tears that tasted
Like his own sweat or the insults of the sea.

Ferryboat

Once at sea, everything is changed:
Even on the ferry, where
There's hardly time to check all the passports
Between the dark shore and the light,
You can buy tax-free whiskey and cigars
(Being officially nowhere)
And in theory get married
Without a priest, three miles from the land.

In theory you may also drown
Though any other kind of death is more likely.
Taking part in a national disaster
You'd earn extra sympathy for your relations.

To recall this possibility the tables and chairs
Are chained down for fear of levitation
And a death's-head in a lifejacket grins beside the bar
Teaching the adjustment of the slender tapes
That bind the buoyant soul to the sinking body,
In case you should find yourself gasping
In a flooded corridor or lost between cold waves.

Alive on sufferance, mortal before all,
Shipbuilders all believe in fate;
The moral of the ship is death.

Marge Piercy

Marge Piercy was born in 1936 in Detroit, Michigan, to working-class parents. The first member of the family to attend college, she went to the University of Michigan on a scholarship and received her B.A. in 1957. One year later she received an M.A. from Northwestern University. Piercy worked at odd jobs for ten years before she was able to support herself as a writer. She began publishing her work during the sixties; her first six novels were rejected, but *Going Down Fast* was published in 1969. Her other publications include the novels *Dance the Eagle To Sleep* (1970), *Small Changes* (1973), *Woman on the Edge of Time* (1976), *Vida* (1980), *Braided Lives* (1982), *Fly Away Home* (1984), and the poetry collections *Breaking Camp* (1968), *To Be of Use* (1972), *The Twelve-Spoked Wheel Flashing* (1978), *The Moon Is Always Female* (1980), *Circles on the Water: Selected Poems* (1982), and *Stone, Paper, Knife* (1983).

As a young woman Piercy was active in the civil rights movement and the SDS (Students for a Democratic Society). Later she became disenchanted with these male-dominated political organizations and became an active feminist. She is often called a political writer because her work contains a vision of the way she believes the world should be and expresses her anger at present injustices. Some critics find her work too polemic, but the power and passion of her novels as well as her poems is widely admired.

The Window of the Woman Burning

Woman dancing with hair
on fire, woman writhing in the
cone of orange snakes, flowering
into crackling lithe vines:
Woman
you are not the bound witch
at the stake, whose broiled alive
agonized screams
thrust from charred flesh
darkened Europe in the nine millions.
Woman
you are not the madonna impaled
whose sacrifice of self leaves her
empty and mad as wind,
or whore crucified
studded with nails.

Woman
you are the demon of a fountain of energy
rushing up from the coal hard
memories in the ancient spine,
flickering lights from the furnace in the solar
plexus, lush scents from the reptilian brain,
river that winds up the hypothalamus
with its fibroids of pleasure and pain
twisted and braided like rope,
like the days of our living,
firing the lanterns of the forebrain
till they glow blood red.

You are the fire sprite
that charges leaping thighs,
that whips the supple back on its arc
as deer leap through the ankles:

dance of a woman strong
in beauty that crouches
inside like a cougar in the belly
not in the eyes of others measuring.

You are the icon of woman sexual
in herself like a great forest tree
in flower, liriondendron bearing sweet tulips,
cups of joy and drunkenness.
You drink strength from your dark fierce roots
and you hang at the sun's own fiery breast
and with the green cities of your boughs
you shelter and celebrate
woman, with the cauldrons of your energies
burning red, burning green.

The Deck That Pouts

My deck is furious.
I took it on six jets,
through hotels, motels
up to timberline
on a snoozing volcano
twitching like a dreaming cat.
I was seeking money
and fleeing trouble
like a storm I could outrun.
Now my cards sing disaster,
bristling swords like a porcupine.
I know it is my own psyche
I fan on the table.
Now I must stand, face upward

in a rain of blood. I must grasp
my decisions like swords.
I must bear them on my back
like wands. I must open
my five senses like doors
to the wind, I must drink down
this salty cup. I am back
in the wreck of my life,
a house a tornado flattened.
I must sleep in the rubble,
my deck under a makeshift pillow.
When we run away, what
we come back to has run
along, and now there is light
where there was shadow
and the colors have shifted brightness.
I rise to rebuild my house
of cards, of paper, here
at the meeting place of winds.

The World Comes Back Like an Old Cat

Slowly the topography emerges, a pile
of thatch from the marsh, a mounded up
rosebush, a pitchfork forgotten several
blizzards ago, rusty tines upthrust from
where its handle froze to the earth,
rows of parsnip and leek still growing,
pellets of owl victims, skull of a vole,
the sharp ears of the crocus: the sun licks
the world into being frenzied with detail
the snow glossed over in its beautiful
monotonous frieze of blue and white marble.

Mornings in Various Years

1.

To wake and see the day piled up
before me like dirty dishes: I have
lived years knitting a love that
he would unravel, as if Penelope
spent every night making a warm
sweater that Odysseus would tear
in his careless diurnal anger.

2.

Waking alone I would marshal my tasks
like battalions of wild geese to bear me
up on the wings of duty over

the checkered fields of other lives.
Breakfast was hardest. I would trip
on ghostly shards of broken
domestic routines that entangled
my cold ankles as the cats yowled
to be fed, and so did I.

3.

I wake with any two cats, victors
of the nightly squabble of who
sleeps where, and beside me, you
your morning sleepyhead big as a field
pumpkin, sleep caught in your fuzzy
hair like leaves. The sun pours in
sweet as orange juice or the rain licks
the windows with its tongue or the snow
softly packs the house in cotton batting
or the wind rocks us on its bellows.
When we wake we move toward each other.
This opal dawn glows from the center
as we both open our eyes and reach out
asking, are you there? You! You're
there, the unblemished day before us
like a clean white ironstone platter
waiting to be filled.

Ascending Scale

Climbing a long open flight of sandstone steps
shallow, interminable under a sun beating the gong
        of my skull,
as if to a sacrificial platform topping an Aztec pyramid
here on the campus of a southern university in August
for a writers' conference, I met myself descending.

The flat dark eyes of a woman a few years older caught
me on brambles, tearing at my orderly advance
        with briefcase,
the scarlet gauze of my new dress floating around me
like love. I winced at her disheveled anger, the heat
bruising her, the want shining out in waves of black light.

She arrived early; she is staying an extra day; she rushes
from workshop to reception, while I operate on the end of
        a long
elastic twanging its overextension. Always rushing back
to you, always a little annoyed to be elsewhere, I work hard
and shake hands with a calm surrounding a vacuum.

If I lose you like a gold earring in a motel room,
if we misplace each other like a book gone out of print,
if we exhaust love with carelessness, forget to change
        the oil
and let it burn out, haul resentments from elsewhere home
        like mean
relatives who move in and take over, then we will fail

as everyone expects. Loss creates the sad woman I
        met climbing
who raked my face for answers that will never sort. That
        wanting
self would be available salted like nuts on a table, gracious

and needy, what the students imagine they want. I know
    better.
The strength they covet and use is rooted in the plentitude
    of love.

Ruth Pitter

Ruth Pitter was born in Ilford, a suburb of London, in 1897. Her parents shared their love of poetry with their children and worked hard to afford a summer cottage in the forest of Hainault where the family could escape the middle-class life of the city. It was in this setting that Pitter wrote her first poem, at the age of five.

After working for the War Office during World War I, Pitter studied handicrafts and opened a shop with her artist-friend Kathleen O'Hara. She has remained in the shop for years, earning a living by selling hand-painted trays. Pitter's first significant collection was *A Mad Lady's Garland* (1935), followed by *A Trophy of Arms* (1936), *The Spirit Watches* (1940), and *Collected Poems* (1968), among other books. She won the Hawthornden Prize(1937), the William E. Heinemann Award (1954), and she was the first woman to receive the Queen's Gold Medal for Poetry (1955). She was a Commander of the British Empire in 1979.

Apology

Have I, you ask, my fate forgot,
This veering mind, this flying breath,
Presumptuously, whose song is not
Ravished by love nor tamed by death?

O no: so deeply have I read
In love and death, I have descried
That Presence where even death lies dead,
And even the Cyprian veils her pride.

The Difference

There in the field hear the voice of the lark day-long
That leaps up loud with his love into the clear grey:
But if the nest were harried
And the mate that he married
Were fled from the place, he must cease from the song:
But you must sing ever in spite of all wrong,
Whatever is lost, strayed, or stolen away.

There by the water behold the beautiful face
Of the flower that looks up into the smile of the day:
But if the spring were failing,
Or the cold wind were wailing,
She would sink, would fall down there, would die in
    her grace:
But you must bloom still in the desolate place,
Whatever is frozen or withered away.

Vision of the Cuckoo

Known by the ear; sweet voice, sour reputation;
Seen now and then at distance, the double bell
Dying along your flight; now secretly
From the small window darkened by the yew
I with the eye possess you and your meaning.

Secure you walk, picking your food under the roses.
The light on the large head is blue,
The wings are netted cinnamon and umber,
The soft dark eye is earthward, the silver belly
Gleams with reflected pink from fallen petals.

I by the world and by myself offended,
Bleeding with outraged love, burning with hate,
Embattled against time my conqueror
In mindbegotten, misbegotten space,
Drink with fierce thirst your drop of absolution.

No love, no hate, no self; only a life,
Blooming in timelessness, in unconceived
Space walking innocent and beautiful;
Guiltless, though myriad-life-devouring;
Guiltless, though tyrant to your fellow-fowls,
You live; and so in me one wound is healed,
Filled with a bright scar, coloured like the roses.

The Serious Child

O which is more, the pleasure or the pain,
    To see the child who knows
At nine years old, the tale of loss and gain,
    The weight of the world's woes:

Joy for the sacrificial love he learns,
    Or grief for light heart lost?
See, in some farthing matter, how he yearns,
    And sighs, and counts the cost!

He feels his weakness, sees the weary road
    That others go, and he,
On slender shoulders taking up his load
    Fares forth as mournfully.

Child, are we lost? and shall we ever find
    The far abode of joy?
Only within, in kingdoms of the mind,
    My little careworn boy.

Sylvia Plath

Sylvia Plath, the daughter of German immigrants, was born in 1932 in Boston, Massachusetts. Her father, Otto, died when Sylvia was eight; this traumatic event affected her throughout the rest of her life. Her mother, Aurelia, encouraged Plath to write stories and poems as a child. As a teenager, she had works published in *Seventeen* magazine and *The Christian Science Monitor*. In 1950 she attended Smith College on a scholarship. She was a brilliant student and was asked to serve as a guest editor of *Mademoiselle* in New York City for a month. However, shortly after she returned home, she suffered a nervous breakdown, attempted suicide, and was hospitalized for a year. Yet she returned to Smith in 1954 and graduated *summa cum laude* in 1955. A fictionalized account of this experience is contained in her novel, *The Bell Jar*, published under a pseudonym in England in 1962 and again posthumously in 1971.

After her graduation from Smith, Plath attended Cambridge University on a Fulbright Scholarship. There she met the poet Ted Hughes, and the two were married in 1956. They briefly lived in the United States while Plath taught at Smith, but they soon returned to England, living first in London and then on a farm in Devon. Plath decided against pursuing an academic career and instead concentrated on writing poetry and raising her two children, both born during the early sixties. When her marriage broke up in 1962, Plath and her children moved to an apartment in London where she wrote prodigiously. Her first collection, *The Colossus*, appeared in England in 1960 and in New York in 1962. These carefully crafted and controlled poems only begin to reveal her obsession with death and her rage at societal expectations, two themes that would become hallmarks of her later work.

During late 1962 and early 1963, Plath wrote poems at a furious pace, often sending letters to her mother about them. However, despite the breakthrough in her work, this had been a difficult period for her personally. She was miserable over her failed marriage and felt uncertain about how she and her children would manage. On February 11, 1963, she ended her life. The poems she had been working on were published posthumously in the volumes *Ariel* (1965), *Crossing the Water* (1971), and *Winter Trees* (1972). The many letters she had written to her mother have been collected in *Letters Home: Correspondence 1950-1963* (1975), edited by Aurelia Schober Plath.

Plath, usually grouped with Anne Sexton and Robert Lowell as one of the "confessional poets," explored her own feelings ruthlessly. Her work boldly portrays her sense of betrayal by father and husband, as well as her turmoil over the conflicting demands of marriage, art, and children—demands that were made unbearable by her compulsive perfectionism. Through a skilled use of language and imagery, these poems transform her experiences into a modern female mythology interwoven with recurring symbols and searing emotions.

Medallion

By the gate with star and moon
Worked into the peeled orange
          wood
The bronze snake lay in the sun

Inert as a shoelace; dead
But pliable still, his jaw
Unhinged and his grin crooked,

Tongue a rose-colored arrow.
Over my hand I hung him.
His little vermilion eye

Ignited with a glassed flame
As I turned him in the light;
When I split a rock one time

The garnet bits burned like
          that.
Dust dulled his back to ocher
The way sun ruins a trout.

Yet his belly kept its fire
Going under the chainmail,
The old jewels smoldering there

In each opaque belly-scale:
Sunset looked at through milk
          glass.
And I saw white maggots coil

Thin as pins in the dark bruise
Where his innards bulged as if
He were digesting a mouse.

Knifelike, he was chaste enough,
Pure death's-metal. The yard-
      man's
Flung brick perfected his laugh.

Spinster

Now this particular girl
During a ceremonious April walk
With her latest suitor
Found herself, of a sudden, intolerably struck
By the birds' irregular babel
And the leaves' litter.

By this tumult afflicted, she
Observed her lover's gestures unbalance the air,
His gait stray uneven
Through a rank wilderness of fern and flower.
She judged petals in disarray,
The whole season, sloven.

How she longed for winter then!—
Scrupulously austere in its order
Of white and black
Ice and rock, each sentiment within border,
And heart's frosty discipline
Exact as a snowflake.

But here—a burgeoning
Unruly enough to pitch her five queenly wits
Into vulgar motley—
A treason not to be borne. Let idiots

Reel giddy in bedlam spring:
She withdrew neatly.

And round her house she set
Such a barricade of barb and check
Against mutinous weather
As no mere insurgent man could hope to break
With curse, fist, threat
Or love, either.

Morning Song

Love set you going like a fat gold watch.
The midwife slapped your footsoles, and your bald cry
Took its place among the elements.

Our voices echo, magnifying your arrival. New statue.
In a drafty museum, your nakedness
Shadows our safety. We stand round blankly as walls.

I'm no more your mother
Than the cloud that distils a mirror to reflect its own slow
Effacement at the wind's hand.

All night your moth-breath
Flickers among the flat pink roses. I wake to listen:
A far sea moves in my ear.

One cry, and I stumble from bed, cow-heavy and floral
In my Victorian nightgown.
Your mouth opens clean as a cat's. The window square

Whitens and swallows its dull stars. And now you try
Your handful of notes;
The clear vowels rise like balloons.

Lady Lazarus

I have done it again.
One year in every ten
I manage it—

A sort of walking miracle, my skin
Bright as a Nazi lampshade,
My right foot

A paperweight,
My face a featureless, fine
Jew linen.

Peel off the napkin
O my enemy.
Do I terrify?—

The nose, the eye pits, the full set of teeth?
The sour breath
Will vanish in a day.

Soon, soon the flesh
The grave cave ate will be
At home on me

And I a smiling woman.
I am only thirty.

And like the cat I have nine times to die.

This is Number Three.
What a trash
To annihilate each decade.

What a million filaments.
The peanut-crunching crowd
Shoves in to see

Them unwrap me hand and foot—
The big strip tease.
Gentleman, ladies,

These are my hands,
My knees.
I may be skin and bone,

Nevertheless, I am the same, identical woman.
The first time it happened I was ten.
It was an accident.

The second time I meant
To last it out and not come back at all.
I rocked shut

As a seashell.
They had to call and call
And pick the worms off me like sticky pearls.

Dying
Is an art, like everything else.
I do it exceptionally well.

I do it so it feels like hell.
I do it so it feels real.
I guess you could say I've a call.

It's easy enough to do it in a cell.
It's easy enough to do it and stay put.
It's the theatrical

Comeback in broad day
To the same place, the same face, the same brute
Amused shout:

"A miracle!"
That knocks me out.
There is a charge

For the eyeing of my scars, there is a charge
For the hearing of my heart—
It really goes.

And there is a charge, a very large charge,
For a word or a touch
Or a bit of blood

Or a piece of my hair or my clothes.
So, so, Herr Doktor.
So, Herr Enemy.

I am your opus,
I am your valuable,
The pure gold baby

That melts to a shriek.
I turn and burn.
Do not think I underestimate your great concern.

Ash, ash—
You poke and stir.
Flesh, bone, there is nothing there—

A cake of soap,

A wedding ring,
A gold filling.

Herr God, Herr Lucifer,
Beware
Beware.

Out of the ash
I rise with my red hair
And I eat men like air.

Totem

The engine is killing the track, the track is silver,
It stretches into the distance. It will be eaten nevertheless.

Its running is useless.
At nightfall there is the beauty of drowned fields,

Dawn gilds the farmers like pigs,
Swaying slightly in their thick suits,

White towers of Smithfield ahead,
Fat haunches and blood on their minds.

There is no mercy in the glitter of cleavers,
The butcher's guillotine that whispers: "How's this, how's this?"

In the bowl the hare is aborted,
Its baby head out of the way, embalmed in spice,

Flayed of fur and humanity.

Let us eat it like Plato's afterbirth,

Let us eat it like Christ.
These are the people that were important—

Their round eyes, their teeth, their grimaces
On a stick that rattles and clicks, a counterfeit snake.

Shall the hood of the cobra appal me—
The loneliness of its eye, the eye of the mountains

Through which the sky eternally threads itself?
The world is blood-hot and personal

Dawn says, with its blood-flush.
There is no terminus, only suitcases

Out of which the same self unfolds like a suit
Bald and shiny, with pockets of wishes,

Notions and tickets, short circuits and folding mirrors.
I am mad, calls the spider, waving its many arms.

And in truth it is terrible,
Multiplied in the eyes of the flies.

They buzz like blue children
In nets of the infinite,

Roped in at the end by the one
Death with its many sticks.

Poppies in July

Little poppies, little hell flames,
Do you do no harm?

You flicker. I cannot touch you.
I put my hands among the flames. Nothing burns.

And it exhausts me to watch you
Flickering like that, wrinkly and clear red, like the skin of a mouth.

A mouth just bloodied.
Little bloody skirts!

There are fumes that I cannot touch.
Where are your opiates, your nauseous capsules?

If I could bleed, or sleep!—
If my mouth could marry a hurt like that!

Or your liquors seep to me, in this glass capsule,
Dulling and stilling.

But colourless. Colourless.

Antonia Pozzi

Antonia Pozzi was born in Milan, Italy, in 1912 and was educated at the University of Milan. She committed suicide at the age of twenty-six. Her poems, which she had been composing since the age of seventeen, were discovered after her death.

Awakening

Risen from who knows what shadows
with effort recovering the sense
of your weight
of your warmth
and the night has nothing
for your trouble
but this mad burst
of black rain
and the shriek of wind at the windows.

Where was God?

(Brenda Webster, tr.)

Canzonetta

Everyone buys his own
unhappiness
where he wishes—

even in a dark shop
austere
among dusty books
liquidated at half price—

useless books—
all the Greek Tragedies—
but if you don't know Greek
anymore—
can you tell me why you
have bought them?

useless books—
Poetry For Children
with colored soldiers—
but if you don't have
children
yourself
can you tell me why
you have bought them?
if you will never have children
anymore

can you tell me for whom
you have
wasted
your money
this way?

everyone buys his own unhappiness

where he wishes
as he wishes
even
here.

(Brenda Webster, tr.)

Landing

Dull swish of runners
over the buried
lake:

behind us
the narrow track
vanishes in a flurry of snow.

Now the sound rises
of an assault in the pass.

A rhythmic screech:
perhaps the icy weeping of the bivouacs
cry of fearful storms;
or the lament of birds
hoarse pant
of slender foxes seen dying—

Are we not going to a landsend?

And when in other garb
I will pause at the warm windows—
(the sled will have carried me off

in the whirl of its bells,
I will have at my shoulders
lights faces songs)

my shadow
will be on the lake
motionless pledge of me
outside—in the cruel
legendary night.

(Brenda Webster, tr.)

Kathleen Raine

Kathleen Raine was born in Ilford, a suburb of East London, in 1897. She was an only child. In later years Raine said that she inherited her intellectual interests from her father, an English master at County High School, and her inspiration to be a poet from her mother, a woman of Scottish descent familiar with many old ballads and legends. Raine was educated at Miss Hutchinson's School in Ilford and at Girton College, Cambridge. She received an M.A. in botany and zoology in 1929.

Raine has lived in London throughout her life except for stays during both world wars in Northumberland, a country whose wild landscape has been a source of inspiration in her poetry. Before her first volume, *Stone and Flower: Poems 1935-1943*, appeared in 1943, she published many poems in periodicals. Since then she has produced the collections *Living in Time* (1946), *The Pythoness and Other Poems* (1949), *The Year One: Poems* (1952), *The Hollow Hill and Other Poems* (1965), *Six Dreams and Other Poems* (1968), *On a Deserted Shore: A Sequence of Poems* (1973), and *The Oracle in the Heart and Other Poems 1975-1978* (1980). She has also written fourteen books of criticism, including four on William Blake, whose mystical and symbolic works have been a great influence on her own. In recent years she has published a three-volume autobiography, *Farewell Happy Fields* (1973), *The Land Unknown* (1975), and *The Lion's Mouth* (1977).

Raine has received many prizes for her poetry and her criticism. She belongs to a tradition of poets, such as Blake and Yeats, who write of a spiritual dimension. Her poems frequently draw on her dreams as a means of expressing this, and she also writes of her personal growth as a woman.

223

Shells

Reaching down arm-deep into bright water
I gathered on white sand under waves
Shells, drifted up on beaches where I alone
Inhabit a finite world of years and days.
I reached my arm down a myriad years
To gather treasure from the yester-millennial sea-floor,
Held in my fingers forms shaped on the day of creation.

Building their beauty in the three dimensions
Over which the world recedes away from us,
And in the fourth, that takes away ourselves
From moment to moment and from year to year
From first to last they remain in their continuous present.
The helix revolves like a timeless thought,
Instantaneous from apex to rim
Like a dance whose figure is limpet or murex, cowrie or golden
    winkle.

They sleep on the ocean floor like humming-tops
Whose music is the mother-of-pearl octave of the rainbow,
Harmonious shells that whisper for ever in our ears,
'The world that you inhabit has not yet been created.'

The Locked Gates

Everywhere the substance of earth is the gate that we cannot
    pass.
Seek in Hebridean isles lost paradise,
There is yet the heaviness of water, the heaviness of stone
And the heaviness of the body I bring to this inviolate place.
Foot sinks in bog as I gather white water-lilies in the tarn,
The knee is bruised on rock, and the wind is always blowing.
The locked gates of the world are the world's elements,
For the rocks of the beautiful hills hurt, and the silver seas drown,
Wind scores deep record of time on the weathered boulders,
The bird's hot heart consumes the soaring life to feather and
    bone,
And heather and asphodel crumble to peat that smoulders on
    crofters' fires.

Kore in Hades

I came, yes, dear, dear
Mother for you I came, so I remember,
To lie in your warm
Bed, to watch the wonder flame:
Burning, golden gentle and bright the light of the living.

With you I ran
To see the roadside green
Leaves and small cool bindweed flowers
Living rejoicing to proclaim
We are, we are manifold, in multitude
We come, we are near and far,

Past and future innumerable, we are yours,
We are you. I listened
To the sweet bird whose song is for ever,
I was the little girl of the one mother.

World you wove me to please a child,
Yet its texture was thinner than light, fleeter
Than flame that burned while it seemed
Leaves and flowers and garden world without end.
Bright those faces closed and were over.

Here and now is over, the garden
Lost from time, its sun its moon
Mother, daughter, daughter, mother, never
Is now: there is nothing, nothing for ever.

The Wilderness

I came too late to the hills: they were swept bare
Winters before I was born of song and story,
Of spell or speech with power of oracle or invocation,

The great ash long dead by a roofless house, its branches rotten,
The voice of the crows an inarticulate cry,
And from the wells and springs the holy water ebbed away.

A child I ran in the wind on a withered moor
Crying out after those great presences who were not there,
Long lost in the forgetfulness of the forgotten.

Only the archaic forms themselves could tell
In sacred speech of hoodie on gray stone, or hawk in air,

Of Eden where the lonely rowan bends over the dark pool.

Yet I have glimpsed the bright mountain behind the mountain,
Knowledge under the leaves, tasted the bitter berries red,
Drunk water cold and clear from an inexhaustible hidden
  fountain.

A Bad Dream

To enact the evil or the good, waking, we say,
The will is free;
In dreams, all we conceive, reality.
No limit there
To what we may do, what must endure to be.

I have born dream-children, living and dead,
Have been in prison, guilty of murder of persons unknown,
Submitted to known and unknown lovers; fled,
Sometimes stood my ground; found myself unclad,
Abandoned, or too late; travelled on railway-journeys up and
  down
The long tracks of night; lost my companions, my luggage or my
  way,
Been carried out to sea, seen galleons drown
With men aboard them, without a qualm.
Once in an aeroplane
That broke up in mid air, faced death, but floated down
Safe on some bright Mediterranean shore.

But an abortion
Of some misbegotten thing I would not own,
Parasite by no will of mine implanted in me

By some inadvertency,
How, when or by whom I did not know,
But for which I was, nevertheless, to blame,
—Yet last night it was so.
I who fear neither death nor sorrow fear the low,
To be dragged down
Where woman lies apathetic under lust,
In unregarded acts perpetuating woe;
And, waking, knew myself debased
In that world where the imagined is the real.

What's done by flesh and blood cannot be undone;
From acts of dream, waking, we are free.
But every life's a dream lived out
And every dream a looking-glass
Where what has been enacted, or may be,
Wears semblance of its reality.
My night's degrading fantasy
I, or some other who is myself
In that humanity all share,
Whose one dream interpenetrates
Under the full tide of sleep
All secret cells of misery or despair,
At some time suffered, to imprint
That record in the dreaming mind
Whose single fall we all enact
Whose undivided guilt we bear.

'I did not mean it,' children cry,
'Not guilty,' thief and murderer plead,
Invoking in that bewildered lie
Some true self innocent of their deed,
Some true self other than we are;
For there is hope that we may be
Forgiven, who know not what we do.
Oedipus, type of human guilt,
Who unawares his father slew,

As many in dream have done unblamed,
Without will's knowledge or consent,
Pleaded man's ignorance of what the gods knew.
Self-knowledge drove him from his throne
To suffer for the unwitting act,
To travel exile's endless way;
And yet, 'Know thyself,' the Greeks say.

But in our time
The ivory gates of sleep are down,
And what Apollo hid from Oedipus,
Freud's censor cancelled from the Book of Life,
We, who would be as gods, must own:
Assume the guilt of unenacted crime
Committed beyond that broken door.
The Angel's voice cries, 'Sleep no more'
And all for us must be despair
And vain our prayer to be forgiven,
Our trust in time's oblivion,
Our hope to reach the golden clime
Unless some sleeper someday wake
As at a trumpet's sound, from what we are
As to each day we wake absolved from dream.

Told in a Dream

'You have a hundred months to live,' I was told in a dream,
The speaker unknown, but the words plain:
Waking into this world, my death nearer than I had known.

What to the immortal signifies number or months or years?
Up and down the light is woven, a golden skein,
But how hold the living clue that runs time out of mind?

I, standing before the superhuman within, above me
Glimpsed and gone, 'It will be enough,' replied,
Pledging my human time to enact a timeless will.

Little is enough, where of each part there is so great a whole;
Myself, or any self, must answer so,
What, of the poem I write, the life that lives me, can I know?

Dahlia Ravikovitch

Dahlia Ravikovitch was born in 1936 in Ramat-Gan, a suburb of Tel Aviv, Israel. She grew up on a kibbutz, went to school in Haifa, and studied English literature at Hebrew University in Jerusalem. She taught high school for a number of years and served for a short time in the Israeli peace movement.

Ravikovitch's ironic humor and use of language are characteristic of contemporary Hebrew poets, but her style has evolved from a romantic tone in her early works to satire, irony, and quiet outrage. Her first volume, *The Love of an Orange* (1959), established her reputation; another major work of hers is *A Dress of Fire* (1979). Ravikovitch also writes children's literature and has translated *Mary Poppins* as well as works of Yeats, Poe, and Eliot into Hebrew.

Time Caught in a Net

And again I was like one of those little girls
with fingernails black from toil
and building tunnels in the sand.
Wherever I looked I saw purple strips.
And many eyes sparkled like silver beads.
Again I was like one of those little girls
who travel one night around the whole world
to China
and Madagascar
shattering dishes and cups
from a surfeit of love,
a surfeit of love,
a surfeit of love.

(Warren Bargad
and Stanley Chyet, trs.)

Tirzah and the Wide World

Take me to the distant northlands,
Take me to the Atlantic,
Put me down amid different people,
People I've never seen before,
There I'll eat wild berry cakes
And speed on a train in Scandinavia.

Take me to the Pacific Ocean,
Put me down amid the brown fish,
Amid the dolphins, sharks, and salmon,
Amid the pelicans dozing on masts,
I won't even bat an eye
When you take me to the Atlantic.

Take me to the crying rivers
And to the destitute shores,
Where kangaroo hunts kangaroo
And both are garbed in striped coats,
Bring me to the kangaroo
And set me down in the forest marsh.

Wait for me in the belly of the ship
And set me up an electric train,
I'll come quickly
To live among different peoples
I'll grin among the strangers
Like a salmon in the sea.
If you cannot give me an ocean
Give me mountains coated with snow.

Set me down among Christian sailors,
Bring me to the Norwegian coasts,
Bring me to the Australian desert
Most wretched desert in the world;

I'll teach the kangaroo
To read and write, religion and math.
Tell these strange people
I'll be with them soon.

Tell them I'll be
In the midst of the sea next year;
Tell them to ready their nets
And pull up for me
Ring after ring.

(Warren Bargad
and Stanley Chyet, trs.)

How Hong Kong Was Destroyed

I'm in Hong Kong.
There's a bay there swarming with snakes.
There are Greeks, Chinamen, and Blacks.
Carnival crocodiles spread their
jaws by the paper lanterns.
Who told you they're carnivorous?
Hordes of people went down to the river.
You've never seen silk like this,
it's redder than poppy petals.

In Hong Kong
the sun rises in the east
and they water the flowers with scented liquids
to enhance their fragrance.
But at night the paper lanterns whip about in the wind
and if someone's murdered they say:

Was it a Black or a Chinaman?
Did he feel much pain?
Then they toss his body in the river
for all the vermin to eat.

I'm in Hong Kong,
and at night the café lights were lowered.
Outside scores of lanterns were torn apart.
And the earth was bursting and boiling
bursting and boiling
and only I knew
there was nothing in the west
and nothing in the east.
And the paper dragon yawned
but the earth kept bursting.
Hordes of enemies will come here
who've never seen silk in their lives.

But little whores still receive their guests
in stained silk gowns
in little lantern-filled cubicles.
Some of them weep in the morning
over their rancid flesh.
And if someone's killed they say:
Wa-as h-he Black or Chinese?
Poor thing, hope he didn't suffer much.
The first of their guests already come at twilight
like thorns in live flesh.

I'm in Hong Kong
and Hong Kong's on the ocean
suspended like a colored lantern on a hook
at the edge
of the world.
Maybe the dragon will
wrap her in red silk
and drop her

into the starry abyss.
Only the little whores will weep into silk
that men are still
are still
pinching their bellies.

I'm not in Hong Kong
and Hong Kong's not in the world.
Where Hong Kong used to be
there's a single pink stain
half in the sky
and half in the sea.

(Warren Bargad
and Stanley Chyet, trs.)

A Private View

Pain is something useless,
I say,
like a worm crawling on fruit
which then turns tasteless.
I know you
I see what your youth was like
and how your face has yellowed.
This is not how heroes are born.

Heroes are something else,
I think,
they're men who don't vegetate.
They fight in the air and on the sea and in Manchuria too.
Always somewhere remote and strange.

My heart goes out to them to the air and to the sea and to Manchuria
 too
but they'd best not set their hearts on medals.
Usually they're fuel for locomotives
as in Manchuria.
And I'm sorry to say they die like dogs.
Pain is something inhuman,
I insist,
I can't imagine any extenuating circumstance.
It's clearly ugliness itself:
someone lost in secret
goes on turning black
turning black and blighted
wifeless, childless.

(Warren Bargad
and Stanley Chyet, trs.)

Poem of Explanations

There are people who know how to love.
And there are people whom it doesn't suit.
There are people who kiss in the street
And there are others who dislike it,
And not only in the street.
I think it's just one strength among others,
It may be an advantage.
Like the rose of Sharon
Which knows how to blossom
Like the lily of the valley
Which chooses its own colors.
You know,

The rose and the lily, when they blossom
They strike you blind.
I'm not saying this to embarrass them,
I know there are others, too.
In my opinion,
Hummingbirds are the most beautiful of birds
But whoever prefers can choose the nightingale.
Still I keep telling myself,
a dodo,
a three-year-old ram,
an apple that won't redden,
it's not me.

(Warren Bargad
and Stanley Chyet, trs.)

Muriel Rukeyser

Muriel Rukeyser was born in 1913 to an affluent family in New York City. She attended Fieldston School, Vassar College, and Columbia University. At Vassar she, Elizabeth Bishop, and Mary McCarthy founded *The Conspirito*, a literary magazine. Rukeyser had many friends among left-wing activists, socialists, and labor organizers, and throughout her career much of her work spoke directly of social injustice.

Rukeyser's first volume of poetry, *Theory of Flight*, appeared in 1935. During the next thirteen years several others followed, including *Mediterranean* (1938), *A Turning Wind* (1939), *Beast in View* (1944), and *The Green Wave* (1948). After World War II, Rukeyser taught at the California Labor School. Then, with the help of wealthy Californian benefactor Henriette Durham, she returned to New York City, where she taught at Sarah Lawrence College and served as vice president of the House of Photography.

After nearly ten years of publishing silence, she produced *Body of Waking* (1958), *The Speed of Darkness* (1968), and *Breaking Open* (1973), among other volumes. The title poem of her last book of new verse, *The Gates* (1976), is based on the poet's experience during a vigil outside the gates of a prison on behalf of a condemned Korean poet. Rukeyser has also produced biographies of the scientists Williard Gibbs (1942) and Thomas Harrot (1971), essays, several children's books, and several translations, including *Selected Poems of Octavio Paz. The Collected Poems of Muriel Rukeyser* appeared in 1978, two years before her death.

Absalom

I first discovered what was killing these men.
I had three sons who worked with their father in the tunnel:
Cecil, aged 23, Owen, aged 21, Shirley, aged 17.
They used to work in a coal mine, not steady work
for the mines were not going much of the time.
A power Co. foreman learned that we made home brew,
he formed a habit of dropping in evenings to drink,
persuading the boys and my husband—
give up their jobs and take this other work.
It would pay them better.
Shirley was my youngest son; the boy.
He went into the tunnel.

>   *My heart   my mother   my heart   my mother*
>   *My heart   my coming into being.*

My husband is not able to work.
He has it, according to the doctor.
We have been having a very hard time making a living since
    this trouble came to us.
I saw the dust in the bottom of the tub.
The boy worked there about eighteen months,
came home one evening with a shortness of breath.
He said, "Mother, I cannot get my breath."
Shirley was sick about three months.
I would carry him from his bed to the table,
from his bed to the porch, in my arms.

>   *My heart is mine in the place of hearts,*
>   *They gave me back my heart, it lies in me.*

When they took sick, right at the start, I saw a doctor.
I tried to get Dr. Harless to X-ray the boys.
He was the only man I had any confidence in,

the company doctor in the Kopper's mine,
but he would not see Shirley.
He did not know where his money was coming from.
I promised him half if he'd work to get compensation,
but even then he would not do anything.
I went on the road and begged the X-ray money,
the Charleston hospital made the lung pictures,
he took the case after the pictures were made.
And two or three doctors said the same thing.
The youngest boy did not get to go down there with me,
he lay and said, "Mother, when I die,
"I want you to have them open me up and
"see if that dust killed me.
"Try to get compensation,
"you will not have any way of making your living
"when we are gone,
"and the rest are going too."

> *I have gained mastery over my heart*
> *I have gained mastery over my two hands*
> *I have gained mastery over the waters*
> *I have gained mastery over the river.*

The case of my son was the first of the line of lawsuits.
They sent the lawyers down and the doctors down;
they closed the electric sockets in the camps.
There was Shirley, and Cecil, Jeffrey and Oren,
Raymond Johnson, Clev and Oscar Anders,
Frank Lynch, Henry Palf, Mr. Pitch, a foreman;
a slim fellow who carried steel with my boys,
his name was Darnell, I believe. There were many others,
the towns of Glen Ferris, Alloy, where the white rock lies,
six miles away; Vanetta, Gauley Bridge,
Gamoca, Lockwood, the gullies,
the whole valley is witness.
I hitchhike eighteen miles, they make checks out.
They asked me how I keep the cow on $2.

I said one week, feed for the cow, one week, the children's
  flour.
The oldest son was twenty-three.
The next son was twenty-one.
The youngest son was eighteen.
They called it pneumonia at first.
They would pronounce it fever.
Shirley asked that we try to find out.
That's how they learned what the trouble was.

> *I open out a way, they have covered my sky with crystal*
> *I come forth by day; I am born a second time.*
> *I force a way through, and I know the gate*
> *I shall journey over the earth among the living.*

He shall not be diminished, never;
I shall give a mouth to my son.

A Game of Ball

On a ground beaten gold by running and
Over the Aztec crest of the sky and
Past the white religious faces of the
Bulls and far beyond, the ball goes flying.

Sun and moon and all the stars of the moon
Are dancing across our eyes like the flight of armies
And the loser dies.   Dark player and bright
Play for the twinned stiff god of life and death.
They die and become the law by which they fight.

Walls grow out of this light, branches out of the stone,

And fire running from the farthest winds
Pours broken flame on these fantastic sands
Where, sunlit, stands the goddess of earth and death,
A frightful peasant with work-hardened hands.

But over the field flash all the colors of summer,
The battle flickers in play, a game like sacrifice.
The sun rides over, the moon and all her stars.
Whatever is ready to eat us, we have found
This place where the gods play out the game of the sky
And bandy life and death across a summer ground.

Then I Saw What the Calling Was

All the voices of the wood called "Muriel!"
but it was soon solved;   it was nothing, it was not for me.
The words were a little like Mortal and More and Endure
and a word like Real, a sound like Health or Hell.
Then I saw what the calling was :   it was the road I traveled,
   the clear
time and these colors of orchards, gold behind gold and the full
shadow behind each tree and behind each slope.   Not to me
the calling, but to anyone, and at last I saw :   where
the road lay through sunlight and many voices and the marvel
orchards, not for me, not for me, not for me.
I came into my clear being;   uncalled, alive, and sure.
Nothing was speaking to me, but I offered and all was well.

And then I arrived at the powerful green hill.

St. Roach

For that I never knew you, I only learned to dread you,
for that I never touched you, they told me you are filth,
they showed me by every action to despise your kind;
for that I saw my people making war on you,
I could not tell you apart, one from another,
for that in childhood I lived in places clear of you,
for that all the people I knew met you by
crushing you, stamping you to death, they poured boiling
    water on you, they flushed you down,
for that I could not tell one from another
only that you were dark, fast on your feet, and slender.
    Not like me.
For that I did not know your poems
And that I do not know any of your sayings
And that I cannot speak or read your language
And that I do not sing your songs
And that I do not teach our children
        to eat your food
        or know your poems
        or sing your songs
But that we say you are filthing our food
But that we know you not at all.

Yesterday I looked at one of you for the first time.
You were lighter than the others in color, that was
    neither good nor bad.
I was really looking for the first time.
You seemed troubled and witty.

Today I touched one of you for the first time.
You were startled, you ran, you fled away
Fast as a dancer, light, strange and lovely to the touch.
I reach, I touch, I begin to know you.

Nelly Sachs

Nelly Sachs, the only daughter of Jewish manufacturer and inventor William Sachs, was born in 1891 and grew up in the prosperous neighborhood of the Tiergarten in Berlin, Germany. As a young girl she loved reading, dancing, and puppetry, and when she began to write, at the age of seventeen, she wrote puppet plays and conventional romantic poetry, which sometimes appeared in newspapers. In 1921 she published a book of stories set in medieval times, *Legends and Tales*, but it did not attract much attention. During the rise of the Nazi Party, Sachs' interests turned to ancient religious writings such as the Old Testament and the Cabala. Finally she was forced to flee Germany to escape deportation to a concentration camp; in 1940, with the help of her friend, Swedish novelist Selma Lagerlof, she and her mother arrived in Stockholm. They were the only surviving members of her family. Sachs lived with her ailing mother in a one-room apartment, supporting them by translating German poetry into Swedish. Her mother died in 1950, and Sachs eventually became a Swedish subject.

Sachs' postwar verse collections, *In the Dwelling of Death* (1947) and *Eclipse of the Stars* (1949), capture the suffering of the Jewish people in Europe during World War II. In the later volumes, such as *And No One Knows Where To Turn* (1957), *Flight and Change* (1958), and *Journey Beyond the Dust* (1961), her tone softens and her scope broadens to include the sufferings of all humanity. Her later works are cryptic and mystical as she searches for a way to understand the horrors she had witnessed.

In 1966 Sachs was awarded the Nobel Prize for Literature, along with Israeli novelist and story writer Shmuel Yosef Agnon. The year before, she received the Peace Prize of German Publishers. Her work has appeared in English translation in the collecions *O the*

Chimneys: Selected Poems (1967) and *The Seeker and Other Poems* (1970). Sachs died in 1970.

O the Chimneys

And though after my skin worms destroy this
body, yet in my flesh shall I see God.
          —Job, 19:26

O the chimneys
On the ingeniously devised habitations of death
When Israel's body drifted as smoke
Through the air—
Was welcomed by a star, a chimney sweep,
A star that turned black
Or was it a ray of sun?

O the chimneys!
Freedomway for Jeremiah and Job's dust—
Who devised you and laid stone upon stone
The road for refugees of smoke?

O the habitations of death,
Invitingly appointed
For the host who used to be a guest—
O you fingers
Laying the threshold
Like a knife between life and death—

O you chimneys,
O you fingers
And Israel's body as smoke through the air!

A Dead Child Speaks

My mother held me by my hand.
Then someone raised the knife of parting:
So that it should not strike me,
My mother loosed her hand from mine.
But she lightly touched my thighs once more
And her hand was bleeding—

After that the knife of parting
Cut in two each bite I swallowed—
It rose before me with the sun at dawn
And began to sharpen itself in my eyes—
Wind and water ground in my ear
And every voice of comfort pierced my heart—

As I was led to death
I still felt in the last moment
The unsheathing of the great knife of parting.

In the Blue Distance

In the blue distance
where the red row of apple trees wanders
—rooted feet climbing the sky—
the longing is distilled
for all those who live in the valley.

The sun, lying by the roadside
with magic wands,
commands the travelers to halt.

They stand still
in the glassy nightmare
while the cricket scratches softly
at the invisible

and the stone dancing
changes its dust to music.

O Sister

O sister,
where do you pitch your tent?

In the black chicken-run
you call the brood of your madness
and rear them.

The cock's trumpet
crows wounds into the air—

You have fallen from the nest
like a naked bird
passers-by eye
the brazenness.

True to your native land
you sweep the roaring meteors
back and forth with a nightmare broom
before the flaming gates of paradise...

Dynamite of impatience
pushes you out to dance
on the tilted flashes of inspiration.

Your body gapes points of view
you recover the lost
dimensions of the pyramids

Birds
sitting in the branches of your eye
twitter to you the blossoming geometry
of a map of stars.

Night unfolds

a chrysalis of enigmatic moss
in your hand

until you hold the wing-breathing butterfly of morning
quivering—
quivering—
with a cry
you drink its blood.

Fleeing

Fleeing,
what a great reception
on the way—

Wrapped
in the wind's shawl
feet in the prayer of sand
which can never say amen
compelled
from fin to wing
and further—

The sick butterfly
will soon learn again of the sea—
This stone
with the fly's inscription
gave itself into my hand—

I hold instead of a homeland
the metamorphoses of the world—

But Look

But look
but look
man breaks out
in the middle of the marketplace
can you hear his pulses beating
and the great city
on rubber tires
girded about his body—
for fate
has muffled
the wheel of time—
lifts itself
on the rhythm of his breathing.

Glassy displays
broken raven-eyes
sparkle
the chimneys fly black flags
at the grave of air.

But man
has said *Ah*
and climbs
a straight candle
into the night.

Line Like

Line like
living hair
drawn
deathnightobscured
from you
to me.

Reined in
outside
I bend
thirstily
to kiss the end of all distances.

Evening
throws the springboard
of night over the redness
lengthens your promontory
and hesitant I place my foot
on the trembling string
of my death already begun.

But such is love—

Redeemed

Redeemed
from sleep
the great darknesses
of the coal forests
will
leap up
shedding
the glittering leaves
of light-years
and reveal their souls—

Naked
worshipper
of lightning
and song of fire
kneeling
thrusting again
with antlers of being-beside-oneself
at the cliffs of beginning
with the wave-mother's
world-encircling music.

You

You
in the night
busy unlearning the world
from far far away
your finger painted the ice grotto
with the singing map of a hidden sea
which assembled its notes in the shell of your ear
bridge-building stones
from Here to There
this precise task
whose completion
is left to the dying.

The Old Couple

The old couple
sitting hand in hand
twin constellation
still glowing with the burnt music
of their past
when they died as they loved—
bewitched by the magic of a black prince
this excised silhouette of night
like insomnia mourning on the retina
while their future in cuticles and hair
outgrows their death—

Anne Sexton

Born in 1928 to an upper middle-class family, Anne Sexton reveals the troubled side of her suburban home life, first as a daughter, then as a wife, in her disturbing and witty poems. She was educated in the public schools of Wellesley, Massachusetts, at Rogers Hall Preparatory School in Lowell, and at Garland Junior College in Boston. In 1948 she eloped with Alfred Sexton; their marriage lasted until 1973. Sexton, the recipient of a scholarship sponsored by the Hart Agency of Boston, modeled occasionally until she became pregnant with her first child.

During the early fifties, after giving birth to two daughters, Sexton had an abortion which caused so deep a depression that she attempted suicide and had to spend the next three years in a sanitarium. On the advice of her psychiatrist, she took courses at Boston University, among them a poetry-writing workshop taught by Robert Lowell. She and Sylvia Plath, also in this class, were both inspired by Lowell's style. In 1960, Sexton published her first book, *To Bedlam and Part Way Back*, which describes the experience of her illness and institutionalization. The books that followed were produced in rapid succession; they include *All My Pretty Ones* (1962), the Pulitzer Prize winning *Live or Die* (1966), *Love Poems* (1969), *Transformations* (1971), *The Book of Folly* (1972), and *The Death Notebooks* (1974). *The Awful Rowing Toward God* (1975) was published posthumously. Not as well-known are the children's books that she co-authored with her close friend, Maxine Kumin, and the two novels that she wrote. She also taught at Harvard, Radcliffe, and Oberlin colleges as well as Boston and Colgate universities.

Sexton, like Sylvia Plath and Robert Lowell, is often described as a "confessional poet," due to her ability to transform her painful life

experiences into art. In spite of the despair that drove her to drug
and alcohol dependence and finally to suicide in 1974, she was a
prolific writer whose work is full of vitality and frankness.

Rowing

A story, a story!
(Let it go. Let it come.)
I was stamped out like a Plymouth fender
into this world.
First came the crib
with its glacial bars.
Then dolls
and the devotion to their plastic mouths.
Then there was school,
the little straight rows of chairs,
blotting my name over and over,
but undersea all the time,
a stranger whose elbows wouldn't work.
Then there was life
with its cruel houses
and people who seldom touched—
though touch is all—
but I grew,
like a pig in a trenchcoat I grew,
and then there were many strange apparitions,
the nagging rain, the sun turning into poison
and all of that, saws working through my heart,
but I grew, I grew,
and God was there like an island I had not rowed to,
still ignorant of Him, my arms and my legs worked,
and I grew, I grew,
I wore rubies and bought tomatoes

and now, in my middle age,
about nineteen in the head I'd say,
I am rowing, I am rowing
though the oarlocks stick and are rusty
and the sea blinks and rolls
like a worried eyeball,
but I am rowing, I am rowing,
though the wind pushes me back
and I know that that island will not be perfect,
it will have the flaws of life,
the absurdities of the dinner table,
but there will be a door
and I will open it
and I will get rid of the rat inside of me,
the gnawing pestilential rat.
God will take it with his two hands
and embrace it.

As the African says:
This is my tale which I have told,
if it be sweet, if it be not sweet,
take somewhere else and let some return to me.
This story ends with me still rowing.

Two Hands

From the sea came a hand,
ignorant as a penny,
troubled with the salt of its mother,
mute with the silence of the fishes,
quick with the altars of the tides,
and God reached out of His mouth
and called it man.
Up came the other hand
and God called it woman.
The hands applauded.
And this was no sin.
It was as it was meant to be.

I see them roaming the streets:
Levi complaining about his mattress,
Sarah studying a beetle,
Mandrake holding his coffee mug,
Sally playing the drum at a football game,
John closing the eyes of the dying woman,
and some who are in prison,
even the prison of their bodies,
as Christ was prisoned in His body
until the triumph came.

Unwind, hands,
you angel webs,
unwind like the coil of a jumping jack,
cup together and let yourselves fill up with sun
and applaud, world,
applaud.

The Earth Falls Down

If I could blame it all on the weather,
the snow like the cadaver's table,
the trees turned into knitting needles,
the ground as hard as a frozen haddock,
the pond wearing its mustache of frost.
If I could blame conditions on *that*,
if I could blame the hearts of strangers
striding muffled down the street,
or blame the dogs, every color,
sniffing each other
and pissing on the doorstep...
If I could blame the war on the war
where its fire Brillos my hair...
If I could blame the bosses
and the presidents for
their unpardonable songs...
If I could blame it on all
the mothers and fathers of the world,
they of the lessons, the pellets of power,
they of the love surrounding you like batter...
Blame it on God perhaps?
He of the first opening
that pushed us all into our first mistakes?
No, I'll blame it on Man
For Man is God
and man is eating the earth up
like a candy bar
and not one of them can be left alone with the ocean
for it is known he will gulp it all down.
The stars (possibly) are safe.
At least for the moment.
The stars are pears
that no one can reach,
even for a wedding.

Perhaps for a death.

Pain for a Daughter

Blind with love, my daughter
has cried nightly for horses,
those long-necked marchers and churners
that she has mastered, any and all,
reigning them in like a circus hand—
the excitable muscles and the ripe neck;
tending this summer, a pony and a foal.
She who is too squeamish to pull
a thorn from the dog's paw,
watched her pony blossom with distemper,
the underside of the jaw swelling
like an enormous grape.
Gritting her teeth with love,
she drained the boil and scoured it
with hydrogen peroxide until pus
ran like milk on the barn floor.

Blind with loss all winter,
in dungarees, a ski jacket and a hard hat,
she visits the neighbors' stable,
our acreage not zoned for barns;
they who own the flaming horses
and the swan-whipped thoroughbred
that she tugs at and cajoles,
thinking it will burn like a furnace
under her small-hipped English seat.

Blind with pain she limps home.

The thoroughbred has stood on her foot.
He rested there like a building.
He grew into her foot until they were one.
The marks of the horseshoe printed
into her flesh, the tips of her toes
ripped off like pieces of leather,
three toenails swirled like shells
and left to float in blood in her riding boot.

Blind with fear, she sits on the toilet,
her foot balanced over the washbasin,
her father, hydrogen peroxide in hand,
performing the rites of the cleansing.
She bites on a towel, sucked in breath,
sucked in and arched against the pain,
her eyes glancing off me where
I stand at the door, eyes locked
on the ceiling, eyes of a stranger,
and then she cries...
Oh my God, help me!
Where a child would have cried *Mama!*
Where a child would have believed *Mama!*
she bit the towel and called on God
and I saw her life stretch out...
I saw her torn in childbirth,
and I saw her, at that moment,
in her own death and I knew that she
knew.

Ntozake Shange

Ntozake Shange was born Paulette Williams on October 18, 1948, in Trenton, New Jersey. Her father was a surgeon and her mother, a psychiatric social worker. The family moved to St. Louis, Missouri, when Shange was eight, and as the oldest of four children she felt the stings of racial hatred most bitterly when bused to a German-American school as part of a desegregation program. However, she immersed herself in literature and the arts and met many celebrated people such as Dizzy Gillespie, Chuck Berry, and Charlie Parker, all of whom were friends of her parents.

Five years later the Williams family returned to New Jersey. In 1966 Shange entered Barnard College, but after one year there she made several suicide attempts, explaining later that the cause had been her suppressed rage against the injustices she had and would have to suffer as a black and as a woman. Nevertheless, she received her B.A. in American Studies from Barnard College in 1970. During the next year she chose the African name by which she is known: Ntozake meaning "she who comes with her own things" and Shange meaning "who walks like a lion." In 1973 she received an M.A. in American Studies from the University of Southern California. For the following three years she taught humanities, women's studies, and Afro-American studies at Mills College, Sonoma State College, and the University of California Extension. At this time she was also combining poetry and dance into dramatic pieces and forming her own theater company called For Colored Girls Who Have Considered Suicide. She moved to New York City where her choreo/poem *For Colored Girls Who Have Considered Suicide When the Rainbow Is Enuf* was produced in 1975. This work, a compilation of twenty poems acted out by seven black female characters, had a long run on Broadway and was highly praised by critics.

Shange has continued to work with drama, writing several more pieces for theater using music and dance, some of which were published in the book *Three Pieces* (1981). Her other books include *Sassafrass: A Novella* (1977), her novels *Sassafrass, Cypress & Indigo* (1982) and *Betsy Brown* (1985), as well as her poetry collections *Nappy Edges* (1978) and *From Okra to Greens* (1984).

& Then
For Jules

is it possible to come
with you and be away from
you/ simultaneously
can i love you and not hold you/
do it seem whatever may/ then also shall
if it's s'posed/ or
is the dragonfly correct in his
assertion that fools are those
who think and believe
then act like they knew
somethin abt livin while death
was inappropriately invited out
to lunch by cajolin rationalizations
wearing star-spangled elekes and
wooing ochun's last/ and fastest
daughter/ maybe not in sight
but in the visions of eyes
larger than our palms
there's a carnival of winged moons
and caring/ and i've
gotta love you and not have you as
a glass covered marble in my
back pocket/ i've gotta love you and

not know you as belonging to an ever
sides glistenin songs rockin
small trees in mossy cradles &
valleys burstin with green lakes in
shade flowers are the only/ binding
and freeness with you one answer
to being and loving with you
an october breeze

Senses of Heritage

my grandpa waz a doughboy from carolina
the other a garveyite from lakewood
i got talked to abt the race & achievement
bout color & propriety/
nobody spoke to me about the moon

daddy talked abt music & mama bout christians
my sisters/ we
always talked & talked
there waz never quiet
trees were status symbols

i've taken to fog/
the moon still surprisin me

Inquiry

my questions concern the subject poetry
is whatever runs out/ whatever digs my guts
til there's no space in myself
cryin wont help/ callin mama wont help
lovers are detours/ no way to assuage this
poem/ but in the words & they are deceitful/
images beat me confuse me/ make me want all of you to share me/
& i hide under my bed/

poetry is unavoidable connection/
some people get married/ others join the Church
i carry notebooks/ so i can tell us what happened/
midnight snacks in bed with whoever/ are no compensation/ when
i'm listenin to multitudes of voices/ i consume yr every word &
move/

durin the day you are initiated into *the holy order
of prospective poems*/ i dream in yr voice/ sometimes act
yr fantasies/ i've made them my own/
whatever is here/ is what you've given me/
if it's not enough for you/
give me some more

Resurrection of the Daughter

the family had been ill for some time
quarantined/socially restricted
to bridge & sunday brunch by the pool
the mother called her daughters twice a day
she saved the son for emergencies
the father drove around a lot
there were no visible scars
under the daughters' biba eyes
lay pain like rachel's/the rage of zelda
delavallades' pirouettes in stasis
the daughters cd set a formal table
curtsey as if not descendants of slaves
& speak english with no accent at all
they were virgins for a long time
one waz on punishment for a month
cuz she closed her eyes while dancin on the wrong
side of town
mama who came from there/knew too well
a cheap pleasure cd spell remorse
for an upwardly mobile girl
& the girl learned well/she paid for her
lovers with her suffering
never knowing some love is due you
she waved her tears in her lover's face
the more there were/the more they were worth
the son looked down on these things
his women did his laundry & his cooking
but they were not crying
the father waz also not crying he waz with ulcers
& waited on the cliffs
where his daughters' lovers prayed for his demise
dyin to be the heads of a sick household
the lovers of the daughters wrought pain
deception & fear wherever they turned

& the son kept his distance
the mother called him in emergencies/occurred all the time
the daughters believed they were ugly dumb & dark
like hades/like mud/like beetles/& filth

the mother washed all the time & kept her kitchen
clean
the father wore perfumes/thot sex a personal decision

a daughter convinced her beauty an aberration
her love a fungus/her womb a fantasy
left the asylum of her home on a hunch
she wd find someone who cd survive tenderness
she wd feed someone who waz in need of her fruits
she wd gather herself an eldorado of her own makin
a space/empty of envy/of hate
she a daughter refused to answer her mother's calls
she refused to believe in the enmity of her sisters
the brother waz callt to see to the emergency
the father bought a new stereo
& she waz last seen in the arms of herself
blushing
having come to herself
in the heat of herself
daughters wait for the wounded to scream themselves
to death
daughters choosin to be women
lick their wounds with their own spit
                                        til they heal

Edith Sitwell

Edith Sitwell was born in 1887 to an aristocratic country family. She and her younger brothers, writers Osbert and Sacheverell Sitwell, grew up on the family estate in Derbyshire, England. Although Sir George Sitwell and Lady Ida Denison arranged for their daughter to be educated at home, this task was accomplished by her grandmother and governess rather than by her parents. In 1914 Sitwell moved to London with her former governess, Helen Rootham.

Sitwell began writing poems at the age of twenty. Her first collection, *The Mother and Other Poems*, did not attract much attention. However, Sitwell soon became known as the editor of and contributor to *Wheels*, an avant-garde literary anthology that appeared annually from 1916 until 1921. The clever, satiric verse that appeared in *Wheels* was a reaction against the rural, nostalgic values of Georgian poetry, which was very popular at that time. The newly emerging poetics, championed by Sitwell, was also affected by the large-scale brutality of the First World War and the growing obsolescence of the old social order. During these years Sitwell produced several volumes of verse, including *Clown's Houses* (1918), *The Wooden Pegasus* (1920), and *Façade* (1922). Sitwell intended for these poems to be read aloud and used words as abstractions to evoke rhythms and melodies of sound. Of the many readings she gave, the best remembered are the dramatic presentations of the poem-sequence *Façade*. Sitwell read these poems from behind a screen, while accompanied by music composed and conducted by William Walton.

Sitwell and Rootham lived in London and Paris until 1938, when Rootham died. In Paris, Sitwell met and fell tragically in love with the surrealist painter Pavel Tchelitchew who was homosexual and did not return her passion. She had many friends and liked to patronize young poets, including Dylan Thomas, whom she discovered, Robert Lowell, Allen Ginsberg, and James Purdy. She had little respect for the work of most women poets with the exception of some works by Sappho, Christina Rossetti, and Emily Dickinson. In her later years, Sitwell continued to produce many books of verse, among the most notable are *Troy Park* (1925), *Gold Coast Customs* (1929), *Street Songs* (1942), and *The Shadow of Cain* (1947). Although she is best known as the author of *Façade*, her later works are markedly different from those early, bright musical experiments; they mourn the end of the way of life remembered from her childhood and look for solace in Catholicism, to which she converted in 1955. Perhaps this conservatism was in part caused by her outrage at social injustices and the horror of the atomic bomb, realities of the modern age she had originally welcomed. Sitwell died in 1964.

Trio for Two Cats and a Trombone

Long steel grass—
The white soldiers pass—
The light is braying like an ass.
See
The tall Spanish jade
With hair black as nightshade
Worn as a cockade!
Flee
Her eyes' gasconade
And her gown's parade
(As stiff as a brigade).
Tee-hee!
The hard and braying light
Is zebra'd black and white,

It will take away the slight
And free
Tinge of the mouth-organ sound,
(Oyster-stall notes) oozing round
Her flounces as they sweep the ground.
The
Trumpet and the drum
And the martial cornet come
To make the people dumb—
But we
Won't wait for sly-foot night
(Moonlight, watered milk-white, bright)
To make clear the declaration
Of our Paphian vocation,
Beside the castanetted sea,
Where stalks Il Capitaneo
Swaggart braggadocio
Sword and moustachio—
He
Is green as a cassada
And his hair is an armada.
To the jade 'Come kiss me harder'
He called across the battlements as she
Heard our voices thin and shrill
As the steely grasses' thrill,
Or the sound of the onycha
When the phoca has the pica
In the palace of the Queen Chinee!

Mariner Man

'What are you staring at, mariner man,
Wrinkled as sea-sand and old as the sea?'
'Those trains will run over their tails, if they can,
Snorting and sporting like porpoises! Flee
The burly, the whirligig wheels of the train,
As round as the world and as large again,
Running half the way over to Babylon, down
Through fields of clover to gay Troy town—
A-puffing their smoke as grey as the curl
On my forehead as wrinkled as sands of the sea!—
But what can that matter to you, my girl?
(And what can that matter to me?)'

Bells of Grey Crystal

Bells of grey crystal
Break on each bough—
The swans' breath will mist all
The cold airs now.
Like tall pagodas
Two people go,
Trail their long codas
Of talk through the snow.
Lonely are these
And lonely am I...
The clouds, grey Chinese geese
Sleek through the sky.

The Drunkard

This black tower drinks the blinding light.
Strange windows, livid white,

Tremble beneath the curse of God.
Yet living weeds still nod

To the huge sun, a devil's eye
That tracks the souls that die.

The clock beats like the heart of Doom
Within the narrow room;

And whispering with some ghastly air
The curtains float and stir.

But still she never speaks a word;
I think she hardly heard

When I with reeling footsteps came
And softly spoke her name.

But yet she does not sleep. Her eyes
Still watch in wide surprise

The thirsty knife that pitied her;
But those lids never stir,

Though creeping Fear still gnaws like pain
The hollow of her brain.

She must have some sly plan, the cheat,
To lie so still. The beat

That once throbbed like a muffled drum

With fear to hear me come

Now never sounds when I creep nigh.
Oh, she was always sly!

And if, to spite her, I dared steal
Behind her bed and feel

With fumbling fingers for her heart...
Ere I could touch the smart,

Once more wild shriek on shriek would tear
The dumb and shuddering air...

Yet still she never speaks to me.
She only smiles to see

How in dark corners secret-sly
New-born Eternity,

All spider-like, doth spin and cast
Strange threads to hold Time fast.

The Greengage Tree

From gold-mosaic'd wave
And from the fountain cave
Grew my dark-plumaged leaves all green and fountain-
    cold,
My minarets of gold,

Mosaic'd like the tomb,
Far in the forest gloom,
Of water-lovely Fatima in forests far away.
The gardener doth sway

The branches and doth find
(As wrinkled dark and kind
As satyrs) these with satyrs' straw beards twined
By that gold-fingered arborist the wind.

Among thick leaves the shade
Seems like a cavalcade,
Or Artemis plume-helmeted from a sylvan serenade,
Or Amazon's ambassade.

A Caliph plays a lute,
A gardener plays a flute,
Then from my feathered stem a most delightful gust,
    a glittering sea
Grows in my rich fruit.

And each bird-angel comes
To sip dark honey from my plums,
My rich green amber gums
That make puffed feather sleeves, long feathered
    skirts all gold,
And sticky from the dew my golden net doth hold.

Dirge for the New Sunrise

Fifteen minutes past eight o'clock, on the morning
of Monday the 6th of August 1945

Bound to my heart as Ixion to the wheel,
Nailed to my heart as the Thief upon the Cross,
I hang between our Christ and the gap where the world
    was lost

And watch the phantom Sun in Famine Street
—The ghost of the heart of Man...red Cain
And the more murderous brain
Of Man, still redder Nero that conceived the death
Of his mother Earth, and tore
Her womb, to know the place where he was conceived.

But no eyes grieved—
For none were left for tears:
They were blinded as the years
Since Christ was born. Mother or Murderer, you have
    given or taken life—
Now all is one!

There was a morning when the holy Light
Was young. The beautiful First Creature came
To our water-springs, and thought us without blame.

Our hearts seemed safe in our breasts and sang to the
    Light—
The marrow in the bone
We dreamed was safe...the blood in the veins, the sap
    in the tree
Were springs of Deity.

But I saw the little Ant-men as they ran
Carrying the world's weight of the world's filth

And the filth in the heart of Man—
Compressed till those lusts and greeds had a greater heat
 than that of the Sun.

And the ray from that heat came soundless, shook the sky
As if in search of food, and squeezed the stems
Of all that grows on the earth till they were dry
—And drank the marrow of the bone:
The eyes that saw, the lips that kissed, are gone
Or black as thunder lie and grin at the murdered Sun.

The living blind and seeing Dead together lie
As if in love....There was no more hating then,
And no more love: Gone is the heart of Man.

Song
To Alberto De Lacerda

Where is all the bright company gone—
The Trojan Elaine and the Knight Sir Gawaine?
Why have they glided out of the rain?
The Queens were bright as the waters' sheen,
Beautiful, bountiful as the grain;
The Knights were brighter than stars in the sky
(The moons thick as roses in hot July)—
As bright as the raindrops and roses in June,
And many and merry as notes in a tune.
Alas, they are gone and I am alone,
For all they glided out of the rain.
And now I sit under the bright apple-tree
And weep that ever the speech was spoken
That the false angel said unto me.
For had I never the apple-branch broken,
Death had not fallen on mankind and me.

Stevie Smith

Florence Margaret Smith was born in Hull, Yorkshire, in 1905. Her parents' marriage was not a happy one. Her father joined the North Sea Patrol when Smith was a little girl, and she seldom saw him. When Smith was three she, her mother, and her sister moved to the unfashionable London suburb of Palmers Green, where the two girls were virtually raised by their "Auntie Lion." Smith, who had tuberculosis when she was five, was a sickly child and was nicknamed Stevie after the famous jockey Steve Donoghue due to her short stature. She graduated from the North London Collegiate School for Girls but did not attend a university. In 1923 she became a secretary at the magazine publishing firm of George Newnes. She worked there until 1953, when she left to take care of her ailing aunt.

Smith's poems first appeared in *Granta* magazine while she was in her twenties. However, her first collection of poems was rejected in 1935 by a publisher who advised her to write a novel instead. She wrote *Novel on Yellow Paper; or Work It Out for Yourself*, which appeared in 1936. This was followed in 1937 by her first volume of poetry, *A Good Time Was Had by All*. These two works established her reputation as a distinctive and truly original voice in British literature. Smith wrote two more novels, *Over the Frontier* (1938) and *The Holiday* (1949), as well as several books of poetry, including *Tender Only to One* (1938), *Mother, What Is Man?* (1942), *Not Waving but Drowning* (1957), *Selected Poems* (1962), and *The Frog Prince and Other Poems* (1966).

In 1969 Smith received the Queen's Gold Medal for Poetry. Recently her life was made the subject of the motion picture *Stevie*, featuring Glenda Jackson. Smith said she read little contemporary poetry, and her work, while certainly modern, is not modeled after any other writer's work. Her poems, sometimes archaic or fairy-tale-

like in tone, are in fact ironic, even tragic, observations of life. Smith
died in 1971.

Thoughts about the Christian Doctrine of Eternal Hell

Is it not interesting to see
How the Christians continually
Try to separate themselves in vain
From the doctrine of eternal pain.

They cannot do it,
They are committed to it,
Their Lord said it,
They must believe it.

So the vulnerable body is stretched without pity
On flames for ever.   Is this not pretty?

The religion of Christianity
Is mixed of sweetness and cruelty
Reject this Sweetness, for she wears
A smoky dress out of hell fires.

Who makes a God? Who shows him thus?
It is the Christian religion does,
Oh, oh, have none of it,
Blow it away, have done with it.

This god the Christians show
Out with him, out with him, let him go.

Away, Melancholy

Away, melancholy,
Away with it, let it go.

Are not the trees green,
The earth as green?
Does not the wind blow,
Fire leap and the rivers flow?
Away melancholy.

The ant is busy
He carrieth his meat,
All things hurry
To be eaten or eat.
Away, melancholy.

Man, too, hurries,
Eats, couples, buries,
He is an animal also
With a hey ho melancholy,
Away with it, let it go.

Man of all creatures
Is superlative
(Away melancholy)
He of all creatures alone
Raiseth a stone
(Away melancholy)
Into the stone, the god,
Pours what he knows of good
Calling good, God.
Away melancholy, let it go.

Speak not to me of tears,
Tyranny, pox, wars,

Saying, Can God
Stone of man's thought, be good?

Say rather it is enough
That the stuffed
Stone of man's good, growing,
By man's called God.
Away, melancholy, let it go.

Man aspires
To good,
To love
Sighs;

Beaten, corrupted, dying
In his own blood lying
Yet heaves up an eye above
Cries, Love, love.
It is his virtue needs explaining,
Not his failing.

Away, melancholy,
Away with it, let it go.

Fafnir and the Knights

In the quiet waters
Of the forest pool
Fafnir the dragon
His tongue will cool

His tongue will cool
And his muzzle dip
Until the soft waters lave
His muzzle tip

Happy simple creature
In his coat of mail
With a mild bright eye
And a waving tail

Happy the dragon
In the days expended
Before the time had come for dragons
To be hounded

Delivered in their simplicity
To the Knights of the Advancing Band
Who seeing the simple dragon
Must kill him out of hand

The time has not come yet
But must come soon
Meanwhile happy Fafnir
Take thy rest in the afternoon

Take thy rest
Fafnir while thou mayest
In the long grass
Where thou liest

Happy knowing not
In thy simplicity
That the knights have come
To do away with thee.

When thy body shall be torn
And thy lofty spirit
Broken into pieces
For a knight's merit

When thy lifeblood shall be spilt
And thy Being mild
In torment and dismay
To death beguiled

Fafnir, I shall say then,
Thou art better dead
For the knights have burnt thy grass
And thou couldst not have fed.

Harold's Leap

Harold, are you asleep?
Harold, I remember your leap,
It may have killed you
But it was a brave thing to do.
Two promontories ran high into the sky,
He leapt from one rock to the other
And fell to the sea's smother.
Harold was always afraid to climb high,
But something urged him on,
He felt he should try.
I would not say that he was wrong,
Although he succeeded in doing nothing but die.
Would you?
Ever after that steep
Place was called Harold's Leap.
It was a brave thing to do.

The Wanderer

Twas the voice of the Wanderer, I heard her exclaim,
You have weaned me too soon, you must nurse me again,
She taps as she passes at each window pane,
Pray, does she not know that she taps in vain?

Her voice flies away on the midnight wind,
But would she be happier if she were within?
She is happier far where the night winds fall,
And there are no doors and no windows at all.

No man has seen her, this pitiful ghost,
And no woman either, but heard her at most,
Sighing and tapping and sighing again,
You have weaned me too soon, you must nurse me again.

Love Me!

Love me, Love me, I cried to the rocks and the trees,
And Love me, they cried again, but it was only to tease.
Once I cried Love me to the people, but they fled like a
    dream,
And when I cried Love me to my friend, she began to scream.
Oh why do they leave me, the beautiful people, and only the
    rocks remain,
To cry Love me, as I cry Love me, and Love me again.

On the rock a baked sea-serpent lies,
And his eyelids close tightly over his violent eyes,
And I fear that his eyes will open and confound me with a

mirthless word,
That the rocks will harp on for ever, and my Love me never
be heard.

Now Pine-Needles

Now pine-needles
You lie under the pine-trees
In the darkness of the pine-trees
The sun has not touched you
You are not brown because the sun has touched you
You are brown because you are dead.
The parent tree sighs in the wind
But it does not sigh for sadness
Only because the wind blows
The pine-tree sighs
Only because you are dead
You are brown.
Well, you do not know
That you were so and so
And are now so and so.
So why should I say
You were alive and are now dead
That your parent tree sighs in the wind?
I will sleep on you pine-needles,
Then I shall be
No more than the pine-tree
No more than the pine-tree's needles.

Gertrude Stein

Gertrude Stein was born in 1874 in Allegheny, Pennsylvania, to a wealthy German-Jewish family. Stein's family lived in Austria and Paris where, as a young child, she learned to speak German and French. The family moved to Oakland, California, when Stein was five years old. When Stein was fourteen, her mother died; her father died just three years later. At that time she and Leo, her older brother with whom she remained very close for years, went to live with their aunt in Baltimore.

When Leo Stein enrolled at Harvard College, Gertrude entered Harvard Annex (which later became Radcliffe College). There she studied philosophy with William James and worked in the Harvard Psychological Laboratory, publishing two technical papers on automatic responses. On James' advice she entered medical school at Johns Hopkins. She did research in neurology and casework in obstetrics in Baltimore's Negro quarter. However, she left after two years without a degree. Leo had gone to Europe to study art, and in 1903 Stein joined him at his Paris residence, 27 rue de Fleurus. She lived in Paris for the rest of her life.

The Steins were great admirers and collectors of modern art. Their home was open to tourists and visiting artists who wished to see works by Henri Matisse, Pablo Picasso, Pierre Bonnard, Juan Gris, Edouard Manet, Paul Gauguin, Paul Cézanne, and Henri de Toulouse-Lautrec. Stein befriended Matisse, Picasso, Georges Braque, and avant-garde writers Max Jacob, Guillaume Apollinaire, and Jean Cocteau. She began to work on her own writing, producing *Q.E.D.* in 1903. This work, about a lesbian relationship she had in Baltimore, was published posthumously in 1950 under the title *Things as They Are*. Stein's first publication was *Three Lives*, which she brought out in America at her own expense in 1909. This nearly "realistic" telling of the lives of three lower-class women was critically acclaimed. From 1906-1911, Stein worked on her lengthy book, *The Making of Americans*, but she did not find a publisher for it until 1925. During this time she also produced "word-portraits" of such famous friends as Picasso and Mabel Dodge. *Tender Buttons* (1914), the volume of poems or poem-like passages, influenced by the cubist movement in painting, was also written at this time.

In the years just before World War I, Stein's close relationship with her brother Leo ended and a lifelong companionship began with Alice B. Toklas, Stein's lover, secretary, and supporter. Stein and Toklas began living together during the final years of the war. Both women served as volunteers for the American Fund for French Wounded, delivering medical supplies in a truck Stein had bought; for this effort she received the Medaille de la Reconnaissance in 1922.

After the war, American and English writers such as Ernest Hemingway, Sherwood Anderson, and F. Scott Fitzgerald were frequent visitors at Stein's home. Although she had close friendships with many writers, the extent to which her own literary theories and practices influenced them is still a matter of controversy. Another of Stein's celebrated friendships, with American composer Virgil Thomson, led to two collaborations: the operas *Four Saints in Three Acts*, first performed in 1934 in Hartford, Connecticut, with an all-black cast, and *The Mother of Us All*, drawn from the life of Susan B. Anthony and first performed in 1947.

The publication of *The Making of Americans* (1925) had not done very well, and that disappointment prompted Stein and Toklas to found their own publishing company, the Plain Edition, which would publish "all the work not yet printed of Gertrude Stein." They printed some of Stein's most difficult and abstract work, such as *How To Write* (1931) and *Operas and Plays* (1932). These volumes, now collector's items, were not commercial successes either.

Stein did become a celebrity, however, with the publication of a series of books based on her own experiences in Europe. In 1933 she wrote her memoir through her friend's perspective, calling it *The Autobiography of Alice B. Toklas*. The work became a bestseller and Literary Guild selection. A well-publicized and successful tour of the United States in 1934 and 1935 provided her with the material for *Everybody's Autobiography* (1937), and *Wars I Have Seen* (1945) recounts her years in the French countryside during World War II.

After the liberation of Paris in December 1944, Stein and Toklas opened their home to American GIs, who became the subject of her book *Brewsie and Willie* (1946). Stein died in 1946 at Neuilly-sur Seine after an operation for stomach cancer and was buried in Pere Lachaise Cemetery. Toklas was buried next to her in 1967.

Critical opinion still varies regarding the value of Stein's most abstract and unconventional work. It was her idea to liberate language from the traditional orderings of space and time by creating a mode of expression, sometimes playfully called "Steinese." This mode of expression is characterized by slightly varied repetitions and the use of words and phrases as abstract patterns of sound and rhythm. Perhaps her most highly regarded poetic works are contained within *Stanzas in Meditation and Other Poems* [*1929-1933*]. These poems are of varying lengths and on a wide variety of topics. Describing her own vision of poetry, Stein wrote in the essay "Poetry and Grammar" (1935) that poems are "concerned with abusing with losing with wanting, with denying with avoiding with adoring with replacing the noun."

Stanzas in Meditation, Sel.

Part I, Stanza XIII

She may count three little daisies very well
By multiplying to either six nine or fourteen
Or she can be well mentioned as twelve
Which they may like which they can like soon
Or more than ever which they wish as a button
Just as much as they arrange which they wish
Or they can attire where they need as which say
Can they call a hat or a hat a day
Made merry because it is so.

Part II, Stanza I

Full well I know that she is there
Much as she will she can be there
But which I know which I know when
Which is my way to be there then
Which she will know as I know here
That it is now that it is there
That rain is there and it is here
That it is here that they are there
They have been here to leave it now
But how foolish to ask them if they like it
Most certainly they like it because they like what they have
But they might easily like something else
And very probably just as well they will have it
Which they like as they are very likely not to be
Reminded that it is more than ever necessary
That they should never be surprised at any one time
At just what they have been given by taking what they have
Which they are very careful not to add with
As they can easily indulge in the fragrance
Not only of which but by which they know

That they tell them so.

Part V, Stanza XLI

I am trying to say something but I have not said it.
Why.
Because I add my my I.
I will be called my dear here.
Which will not be why I try
This which I say is this.
I know I have been remiss
Not with a kiss
But gather bliss
For which this
Is why this
Is nearly this
I add this.
Do not be often obliged to try.
To come back to wondering why they began
Of course they began.

A Frightful Release

A bag which was left and not only taken but turned away was not found. The place was shown to be very like the last time. A piece was not exchanged, not a bit of it, a piece was left over. The rest was mismanaged.

A Purse

A purse was not green, it was not straw color, it was hardly seen and it had a use a long use and the chain, the chain was never missing, it was not misplaced, it showed that it was open, that is all that it showed.

A Mounted Umbrella

What was the use of not leaving it there where it would hang what was the use if there was no chance of ever seeing it come there and show that it was handsome and right in the way it showed it. The lesson is to learn that it does show it, that it shows it and that nothing, that there is nothing, that there is no more to do about it and just so much more is there plenty of reason for making an exchange.

Eye Glasses

A color in shaving, a saloon is well placed in the centre of an alley.

A Cutlet

A blind agitation is manly and uttermost.

Water Raining

Water astonishing and difficult altogether makes a meadow and a stroke.

A Sound

Elephant beaten with candy and little pops and chews all bolts and reckless reckless rats, this is this.

A Table

A table means does it not my dear it means a whole steadiness. Is it likely that a change.

A table means more than a glass even a looking glass is tall. A table means necessary places and a revision a revision of a little thing it means it does mean that there has been a stand, a stand where it did shake.

Suppose an Eyes

Suppose it is within a gate which open is open at the hour of closing summer that is to say it is so.

All the seats are needing blackening. A white dress is in sign. A soldier a real soldier has a worn lace a worn lace of different sizes that is to say if he can read, if he can read he is a size to show shutting up twenty-four.

Go red go red, laugh white.

Suppose a collapse in rubbed purr, in rubbed purr get.

Little sales ladies little sales ladies little saddles of mutton.

Little sales of leather and such beautiful beautiful, beautiful beautiful.

Rhubarb

Rhubarb is susan not susan not seat in bunch toys not wild and laughable not in little places not in neglect and vegetable not in fold coal age not please.

What Is the Name of a Ring

A holder.
A cigarette holder.
Aluminium.
Also platinum.
Thank you so much.
Have we been praised.
We have been praised again.
I do not dare to despair.
Oh no you are very happy.
How well you read me.
And the automobile.
Indeed you do me justice.
I am very happy in winter.
And in summer too.
We go soon.
And enjoy it.
And we are eager.
And resolute.
Then we will have success.
There you are right.
Can you see me swimming.
No but being in a pleasant country.
In an automobile.

That is what I feel.
In this way you can say.
We enjoy the day.

A Poetical Plea

I would like a photograph of that said Captain Dyar.
Of what.
Of villages.
Of villages of course.
I need the money to give away.
To the mutilés and the reformés.
The reformés of the war.
Let us do arithmetic.
Let us do the arithmetic.
Can you see how many days in the year.
Answer. Three hundred and sixty five.
There are double that number alive.
This is the way we sing.
If the government gives separation allowance they can live.
If the husband comes home and they have a pension they can't
live.
Do you see.
Why not.
Because the man is sick and he makes it less.
But you must not be stupid.
We need the money to give away.
To the mutilés and the reformés.
The reformés of the war.
In this way we must.
Excuse me.
In this way they must

You excuse me.

A Sonnet

To the wife of my bosom
All happiness from everything
And her husband.
May he be good and considerate
Gay and cheerful and restful.
And make her the best wife
In the world
The happiest and the most content
With reason.
To the wife of my bosom
Whose transcendent virtues
Are those to be most admired
Loved and adored and indeed
Her virtues are all inclusive
Her virtues her beauty and her beauties
Her charms her qualities her joyous nature
All of it makes of her husband
A proud and happy man.

Marina Tsvetayeva

Marina Tsvetayeva was born in 1892 in Moscow, Russia. Her father was a professor at Moscow University, and her mother was a pianist who died in 1906. As a child she was encouraged by her mother to study music, but Tsvetayeva pursued her own interest in poetry after her mother's death. Her first volume, published in 1910, was praised for its stark, down-to-earth quality.

Tsvetayeva married publisher Sergei Efron in 1912. She and her husband sided with the White (anti-Bolshevik) Army during the Russian civil war and immigrated to Prague in 1922. They lived there and in Paris for several years, impoverished and isolated from other Russian émigrés. Tsvetayeva was considered suspect by the Soviets because she kept close ties with Russian poets, such as Boris Pasternak, who were still living in the U.S.S.R. Meanwhile, her husband, Efron, had changed his allegiance, becoming actively pro-Soviet. He returned to the Soviet Union in 1937. Two years later when Tsvetayeva went to join him, she found he had been arrested and then executed by the government. For the next two years she managed to make a living in the Soviet Union as a translator. In 1941, as the German army advanced across Russia, she was evacuated to Yelabuga, a small town in the Tartar Republic. She hung herself on August 31, 1941.

Though Tsvetayeva's adult life was characterized by poverty and alienation, she remained deeply dedicated to her poetry. It is said by her daughter that she put the demands of her work above all else in her life. The result is poetry written in short, staccato lines and filled with original, direct, and powerful images. She is now regarded as one of the major poets of this century.

Where Does This Tenderness Come From?

Where does this tenderness come from?
These are not the—first curls I
have stroked slowly—and lips I
have known are—darker than yours

as stars rise often and go out again
(where does this tenderness come from?)
so many eyes have risen and died out
    in front of these eyes of mine.

and yet no such song have
I heard in the darkness of night before,
(where does this tenderness come from?):
    here, on the ribs of the singer.

Where does this tenderness come from?
And what shall I do with it, young
sly singer, just passing by?
Your lashes are—longer than anyone's.

          (Elaine Feinstein, tr.)

Poems for Akhmatova

1

Muse of lament, you are the most beautiful of
    all muses, a crazy emanation of white night:
and you have sent a black snow storm over all Russia.
    We are pierced with the arrows of your cries

so that we shy like horses at the muffled
    many times uttered pledge—Ah!—Anna
Akhmatova—the name is a vast sigh
and it falls into depths without name

and we wear crowns only through stamping
    the same earth as you, with the same sky over us.
Whoever shares the pain of your deathly power will
    lie down immortal—upon his death bed.

In my melodious town the domes are burning
    and the blind wanderer praises our shining Lord.
I give you my town of many bells,
    Akhmatova, and with the gift: my heart.

2

I stand   head in my hands   thinking how
    unimportant are the traps we set for one another
I hold my head in my hands   as I sing
    in this late hour, in the late dawn.

Ah how violent is this wave which has
    lifted me up on to its crest: I sing
of one   that is unique among us
    as the moon is   alone in the sky,

that has flown into my heart like a raven,
    has speared into the clouds
hook-nosed, with deathly anger: even
    your favour is   dangerous,

for you have spread out your night
    over the pure gold of my Kremlin itself
and have tightened my throat with the pleasure
    of singing   as if with a strap.

Yes, I am happy, the dawn never
    burnt with more purity, I am
happy to give everything to you
    and to go away   like a beggar.

for I was the first to give you—
    whose voice   deep darkness!   has
constricted the movement of my breathing—
    the name of the Tsarskoselsky Muse.

3

I am a convict. You won't fall behind.
You are my guard. Our fate is therefore one.
And in that emptiness that we both share
the same command to ride away is given.

And now my demeanour is calm.
And now   my eyes are without guile.
Won't you set me free, my guard, and
let me walk now, towards that pine-tree?

4

You block out everything, even the sun
    at its highest, hold all the stars in your hand!
If only through—some wide open door, I

could blow like the wind to where you are,

and starting to stammer, suddenly blushing,
   could lower my eyes before you
and fall quiet, in tears, as
   a child sobs to receive forgiveness.

(Elaine Feinstein, tr.)

Readers of Newspapers

It crawls, the underground snake,
crawls, with its load of people.
And each one   has his
newspaper, his skin
disease; a twitch of chewing;
newspaper *caries*.
Masticators of gum,
readers of newspapers.

And who are the readers? old men? athletes?
soldiers? No face, no features,
no age. Skeletons—there's no
face, only the newspaper page.

All Paris   is dressed
this way from forehead to navel.
Give it up, girl, or
you'll give birth to
a reader of newspapers.

Sway/ he lived with his sister,

Swaying/ he killed his father,
They blow themselves up with pettiness
as if they were swaying with drink.

For such gentlemen   what
is the sunset or the sunrise?
They swallow emptiness,
these readers of newspapers.

For news   read: calumnies,
For news   read: embezzling,
in every column   slander
every paragraph some   disgusting thing.

With what, at the Last Judgement
will you come before the light?
Grabbers of small moments,
readers of newspapers.

Gone! lost! vanished! so,
the old maternal terror.
But mother, the Gutenberg Press
is more terrible than Schwarz' powder.

It's better to go to a graveyard
than into the   prurient
sickbay of scab-scratchers.
these readers of newspapers.

And who is it rots our sons
now in the prime of their life?
Those corrupters of blood
the *writers* of newspapers.

Look, friends   much
stronger than in these lines, do
I think this, when with

a manuscript in my hand

I stand before the face
there is no   emptier place
than before the absent
face of an editor of news
                papers' evil filth.

(Elaine Feinstein, tr.)

Fadwa Tuquan

Fadwa Tuquan was born in 1917 to a family of poets and intellectuals in the village of Nablus, Palestine, now part of the territory controlled by Israel. She was one of the leaders of the modernist movement in Arab poetry; her work is considered innovative in both subject matter and form. Since the Six-Day War in 1967, Tuquan's poetry has become increasingly political. Her publications include *I Have Found It* (1962) and *The Guerilla and the Land* (1968).

Behind Bars, Sel.

I

My mother's phantom hovers here
her forehead shines before my eyes
like the light of stars
She might be thinking of me now,
dreaming
> (Before my arrest
> I drew letters in a book
> new and old
> I painted roses
> grown with blood
> and my mother was near me
> blessing my painting)
I see her
on her face silence and loneliness now

and in the house
silence and loneliness
My satchel there on the bookshelf
and my school uniform
on the hanger
I see her hand reaching out
brushing the dust from it
I follow my mother's steps
and listen to her thoughts
yearn to her arms and the face of day

(Hatem Hussaini, tr.)

After Twenty Years

Here the foot prints stop;
Here the moon
Lies with the wolves, the dogs, and the stones,
Behind the rocks and the tents, behind the trees.
Here the moon
Sells its face every night,
For a dagger, a candle, a braid of rain.
Don't throw a stone in their fire;
Don't steal the glass rings
From the gypsies' fingers.
They slept, and so did the fish and the stones and the trees.

Here the foot prints stop;
Here the moon was in labour.
Gypsies!
Give her then the glass rings
And the blue bracelets.

(translated from Arabic, translator unknown)

I Won't Sell His Love

What chance
Sweet dreamlike chance
Joined us here in this distant land
Here two strange souls we
Were united by the Muse
Who carried us away
Our souls becoming a song
Floating on a Mozart air
In its precious world

You said: How deep your eyes
How sweet you are
You said it with hushed, echoing desire
For we were not alone
And in your eyes an invitation
And in my depths intoxication
What intoxication
I am a woman so forgive my heart its vanity
When your murmur caresses it: How deep your eyes
How sweet you are

O Poet, in my country
My beloved country
I have a sweetheart waiting
He is my countryman I won't squander
His heart
He is my countryman I won't sell
His love
For the world's treasures
For the shining stars
For the Moon
Yet intoxication grips my heart
As in your eyes drift love's shadows
Or invitation glimmers

I am a woman so forgive my heart its vanity
When your murmur caresses it: How deep your eyes
How sweet you are

(Mounah Aikhouri
and Hamid Algar, trs.)

Miriam Waddington

Miriam Waddington was born Miriam Dworkin, a member of an intellectual Jewish family in Winnipeg, Canada, in 1917. In 1939 she received a B.A. at the University of Toronto and then studied social work in Toronto and Philadelphia. She married Patrick Waddington and had two sons; the couple later divorced. In 1945 she moved to Montreal and became active in social work and literary life. She returned to Toronto in 1960 and began to work for the North York Family Service. In 1964 she joined the English Department at York University and taught there until her retirement in 1983.

Waddington began writing poems as a child; many of her early works appeared in high school and college publications. Her first volume of poetry, *Green World*, was published in 1945. She has since produced many volumes of poetry, including *The Second Silence* (1955), *The Glass Trumpet* (1966), *Say Yes* (1969), *Mister Never* (1978), and *The Visitants* (1981). Her publications also include a book of short stories, *Summer at Lonely Beach and Other Stories* (1982), as well as critical works and essays.

The Milk of the Mothers

Stars, stars,
lean down and speak:
tell me what I am
on mother earth,
our planet.

They have reduced
our winnowing skies
to ash and lava,
and set out lunar
onion plants with
mountain parsley;
without a word they
rolled our mother
earth, this planet,
in syrups of the dead.

Crumbs of recent
feudal feasts
still cling to our
nuclear shrouds,
and one-dimensional
graphic cows are
outlined stiff in
charcoal to mark
the shadowy shifting
negatives of field
and forest.

No grave
delineates the light
of absent earth,
and there is no one
left to hear

the cries of those
whose ashes are
heaped green and
pulsing in deserted
tomato fields.

Tell me, stars,
what fortune-teller
will now guess
the thoughts of
weather and what
wizard bind the
splintered sides
of logged-over
blackened hills?

Stars, the milk
of the old mothers
is thin and the
milk of the young
mothers is shrieking;
the milk of the
mothers runs out
from every eye and
breast and throbs
with the white blood
of electricity.

Stars, stars,
lean down and speak!
Tell me what I am,
and tell me where
is the milk of
all the mothers now
on earth, our planet?

How Old Women Should Live

Old women
should live like worms
under the earth,
they should come out
only after a good rain.

Or be the kind of worm
that lives in flour
that has stood too long
and when discovered
is thrown away in disgust
by the good housewife.

Or be a wood-worm
that patiently winds
its journey through
history's finest
furniture like those
old women we see
in the corridors of
nursing homes.

Or they should be
constructive like the
silk-worm who lives
on nothing but a box
of mulberry leaves in
hot China too far away
to bother anyone.

The wisest old women
imitate the glow-worm
who is never seen by day
with all its grey worminess

and shrivelled feet,
but shines wise and warm
only after dark.

Old women should be
magical like those worms
in transition and chrysalis
from egg to butterfly;
even decrepit old women
can turn into butterflies
in the third existence
promised to us all.

And remember that worms
are fussy about where
they live and what they eat;
they like warmth, darkness,
and good nourishment and
sometimes when it suits them
they like to come out in
all their loose nakedness
to crawl in the sun.

Past the Ice Age

All of a sudden
I was empty spaces,
flexible snow
wrapping the air.

All of a sudden
I was ropes of night,
crickets of song
under cellar stairs.

I was a lap of
strawberries a stand
of cornflowers a
glassful of ice

And I wanted to
live a long time
just to hear
the new music
in everything.

Lady in Blue: Homage to Montreal

Lady in the blue
dress with the
sideward smile,
I see you at your
easel in the field
beside your house
painting the blur
of long-ago summer
in the night-eyes
of children in the
dark mouths of
sleepwalkers in the
floating bodies
of rock-throwers
and flame-eaters.

In the soundless
streets of our French
bedlam city with
its old creaking
heart and venereal
stairways, its bridges,
spaghetti houses, railway
hotels and second-hand
monuments, there,
Lady Blue of the
saint suburbs, there,
just there you were
lost, lost under
the mountain, under
the snows and calèches,
the steep cliffs of
Côte des Neiges, there
you were lost under

the fortress façades
of a thousand steel-
armoured apartments.

Under the slow blonde
sorrows of your tangled
hair we are all lost,
lost in the distance of
endless streets in the
trackless wastes of our
vanished mother-city;
we are ghost people,
uneasy night-walkers
locked up in Montreal,
and we will never leave
unless your tireless
brush moves us and draws
us into the blue-sleeved
avenues of your still-
flowing rivery wonder.

The Visitants

At night you think
of your friends the dead;
they sing to you
in a choir of stone voices
and you want to tell them
old stories more ancient
than you mortally know,
all that you fleetingly
surmise shimmering
through the hole
in the foliage of the
nearest tree.

Oh those voices of stone!
Those earth-stained voices
those murmurings in wood
those singings in grasses
those soundings and turnings
on the pathless prairie;
my father groaning and
Gabriel Dumont staring
blindly into the camera
of his own fate.

Those anguished visitants:
they come to dissolve
the emptiness,
they come to console
your cries they come
with their firefly lanterns
to lead you amazed
through their blazing
gateways of stone.

Diane Wakoski

Diane Wakoski was born in 1937 in Whittier, California. Reticent by nature, it is only through her poetry that we know she was one of two daughters born to poor Polish-American parents, and that her father deserted the family while she was still quite young. She studied music and poetry at the University of California, Berkeley, receiving a B.A. in 1960. That same year she moved to New York City, where she worked in a bookstore and taught English at a junior high school. She has been married three times, most recently in 1982 to Robert J. Turney.

Wakoski is the author of numerous books of verse, including such titles as *Coins and Coffins* (1962), *The George Washington Poems* (1967), *Inside the Blood Factory* (1968), *The Motorcycle Betrayal Poems* (1971), *Waiting for the King of Spain* (1976), *The Man Who Shook Hands* (1978), *The Lady Who Drove Me to the Airport* (1982), and *The Complete Greed, Parts 1-13* (1984). Her latest book is *The Rings of Saturn* (1986).

George Washington Sends a Pair of
Shoebuckles to the Buddha on His Birthday

Sages
walk
barefoot
sometimes

thru history

as do patriots and soldiers
when they don't
have shoes.

But in case,
Dear Sir,
you are ever thinking
of appearing
formally,
a pair of shoe buckles
might be
in order.

My Lord,
I would give as much
to
any man.

The Elephant & the Butterfly Meet
on the Buddha's Birthday

As the blue wings
brush by
the large grey dusty ear,
wrinkled and soft as a dried peach,
the butterfly
engages in
flickering reflection:
>   no danger here.
>   Because I couldn't be still long enough
>   to be crushed

The elephant
says he would like to visit her
in her own home.
This being too whimsical for the butterfly
she moves on.
A Camera.
A Secret.
A Way of looking at things.

I find certain subjects
sentimental;
the prison my face locks me in.

Sun Gods Have Sun Spots

I dont care if you are
the sun god;
the flames leaping out of your eyes
flash,
turn green,
remind me that I might be looking at the god of rattlesnakes
those tongues of fire and light we see
dancing on the sun.

And if you are consumed by your own fire
And if you are a dying star
And if you are so active on the tennis courts
And if you have 12 girl friends
And if you are 6 feet tall
And if you are Russian
And if you drive a Mercedes
I dont care about any of those things.

Because I know this secret.
I am
also a ruler of the sun,
I am the woman
whose hair lights up a dark room,
whose words are matches
who is a lion
on fire,
         burning in the woods,
at night.
Women
they say
keep
the home-fires
burning.
         The first man to land

on the sun
will scorch his feet.

A Valentine for Ben Franklin Who Drives a Truck in California

I cut the deck
and found a magician
driving a mack truck
down the California grapevine.
His eyes were glistening Japanese beetles,
and his hands were surveyors of the moon.
He pulled a carnation
out of his sleeve,
and offered me a ride.
I took the flower and said I was leaving
to be an illusionist. He said
he specialized in cards
and sleight of hand.
I touched his mouth and ears
with my lips,
                "Keep on truckin,"
I said.
But he laughed and told me a bedtime story.
His body was an elm.
His mouth was filled with grapes.
His hands turned my body into new honey.

Now I am home alone,
reading directions
for sawing a beautiful woman in half.
First you start with a mirror. . .

Before I turn down
the crisp sheets of my bed,
I shuffle the tarot deck.
But the magician is missing.
Is he
still driving the freeways of California?
Or is he
only an illusion
in my own
magician's
head?

The Ring

I carry it on my keychain, which itself
is a big brass ring
large enough for my wrist,
holding keys for safe-deposit box,
friends' apartments,
my house, office and faithless car.

I would like to wear it,
the only ornament on my plain body,
but it is a relic,
the husband gone to other wives,
and it could never be a symbol of sharing,
but like the gold it's made of, stands for possession, power,
the security of a throne.

So, on my keyring,
dull from resting in my dark purse,
it hangs, reminding me of failures, of beauty I once had,

of more ancient searches for an enchanted ring.

I understand, now, what that enchantment is, though.
It is being loved.
Or, conversely, loving so much that you feel loved.
And the ring hangs there
with my keys,
reminding of failure.

This vain head full of roses,
crystal,
bleeding lips,
a voice doomed to listen, forever,
to itself.

Tearing up My Mother's Letters

The rain of summer thunders down past the sweet peas
trailing up the staves
of my balcony,
and I,
just returned from a journey,
am sitting among pencils and letters and checkbooks,
thinking of the pleasures of sleeping
in my own bed tonight,
wondering if my yellow roses like this rain,
for "roses," as a good poet has said, "are heavy feeders,"
and I'm wishing I were with a certain man,
let us call him "Michael," for that name is common, and as good
as any other,
but I am alone, as usual,
taking the pleasures one has in solitude,

of music and books,
letters from/to friends,
a good glass of wine,
and I notice that I write the checks first, to pay
my bills,
then I write to my mother,
from whom I am often estranged,
and that, unlike all my other pieces of mail, which I file,
as I answer (or decide not to answer), I tear up
my mother's letter
in her fine bookkeeper's handwriting,
recalling that I have always saved most friends' letters,
but always torn up family ones.

Just a note.
The rain has stopped. I
go out on the balcony to check my plants. The sweet peas
are leaning out into the night. Lightning flashes quickly,
like the pain which slithers in and out of my right knee during
cross-country drives.
I tear up my mother's letters
because she is a sad woman and has given me
the gift of her sadness.
The words so thin and determined,
reminding me of how seriously we all take our small lives.
And I am ashamed of her letters;
they could be written by me,
that part of me I could never love,
that small, frightened, even stupid part,
determined to be noticed,
when it should rejoice in being ignored.
That too-loud voice which always embarrasses me
in a quiet room.

I tear up her letters
as I have tried to tear that part
out of me.

Judith Wright

Judith Wright was born in 1915 in Armidale, New South Wales, Australia, to a sheepherding family who had settled in the area during the 1820s. She was educated at the New England Girls School in Armidale and at the University of Sydney. After visiting Europe during the late twenties, she settled in Sydney, but at the start of World War II she returned to the family property in Wallamumbi. This stay at her childhood home provided the inspiration for many of her early works.

Wright was an honors tutor in English at the University of Queensland from 1944 to 1948, and during this time she married J.P. McKinney, a philosopher and writer. They had one daughter. During the sixties, Wright became active in the anti-war and conservationist movements. She now lives in a wildlife sanctuary near Braidwood.

Wright published her first volume of poetry, *The Moving Image*, in 1946. Other important volumes include *Woman to Man* (1949), *Birds* (1962), and *The Double Tree: Selected Poems 1942-1976* (1978). She has also written children's fiction, a book of short stories, and a book of criticism, *Preoccupations in Australian Poetry* (1965). *The Coral Battleground* (1977) is a description of her struggle to protect the Great Barrier Reef from oil drills and limestone mines.

Wright's first work was greeted with great enthusiasm by Australian critics, who praised its honesty, beauty, and craftsmanship. In later years, Wright's verse has become more abstract, and for the most part these efforts have not been as well received. Nevertheless, she is considered to be among Australia's most respected, prolific, and diverse poets.

Blue Arab

The small blue Arab stallion dances on the hill
like a glancing breaker, like a storm rearing in the sky.
In his prick-ears the wind, that wanderer and spy,
sings of the dunes of Arabia, lioncoloured, still.

The small blue stallion poses like a centaur-god,
netting the sun in his sea-spray mane, forgetting
his stalwart mares for a phantom galloping unshod;
changing for a heat-mirage his tall and velvet hill.

Woman to Man

The eyeless labourer in the night,
the selfless, shapeless seed I hold,
builds for its resurrection day—
silent and swift and deep from sight
foresees the unimagined light.

This is no child with a child's face;
this has no name to name it by:
yet you and I have known it well.
This is our hunter and our chase,
the third who lay in our embrace.

This is the strength that your arm knows,
the arc of flesh that is my breast,
the precise crystals of our eyes.
This is the blood's wild tree that grows
the intricate and folded rose.

This is the maker and the made;
this is the question and reply;
the blind head butting at the dark,
the blaze of light along the blade.
Oh hold me, for I am afraid.

Woman to Child

You who were darkness warmed my flesh
where out of darkness rose the seed.
Then all a world I made in me;
all the world you hear and see
hung upon my dreaming blood.

There moved the multitudinous stars,
and coloured birds and fishes moved.
There swam the sliding continents.
All time lay rolled in me, and sense,
and love that knew not its beloved.

O node and focus of the world;
I hold you deep within that well
you shall escape and not escape—
that mirrors still your sleeping shape;
that nurtures still your crescent cell.

I wither and you break from me;
yet though you dance in living light
I am the earth, I am the root,
I am the stem that fed the fruit,
the link that joins you to the night.

For My Daughter

The days begin to set
your difference in your face.
The world has caught you up
to go at the world's pace.
Time, that is not denied,
as once from my heart it drew
the blood that nourished you,
now draws you from my side.

My body gave you then
what was ordained to give,
and did not need my will.
But now we learn to live
apart, what must I do?
Out of my poverty
what new gift can there be
that I can find for you?

Love was our first exchange—
the kindness of the blood.
Animals know as much,
and know that it is good.
But when the child is grown
and the mouth leaves the breast,
such simple good is past
and leaves us more alone.

So we grow separate
and separate spend our days.
You must become your world
and follow in its ways;
but out of my own need,
not knowing where nor how,
I too must journey now

upon a different road.

While love is innocent
the lion walks beside.
But when the spell's undone
and where the paths divide,
he must be tamed, or slain,
or else the heart's undone.
The path I walk upon
leads to his den again.

When I shall meet with him
I pray to wrestle well;
I pray to learn the way
to tame him, not to kill.
Then he may be my friend,
as Una's once, in love,
and I shall understand
what gifts are mine to give.

The Other Half

The self that night undrowns when I'm asleep
travels beneath the dumb days that I give,
within the limits set that I may live,
and beats in anger on the things I love.
I am the cross it bears, and it the tears I weep.

Under the eyes of light my work is brief.
Day sets on me the burdens that I carry.
I face the light, the dark of me I bury.
My silent answer and my other half,
we meet at midnight and by music only.

Yet there's a word that I would give to you:
the truth you tell in your dumb images
my daylight self goes stumbling after too.
So we may meet at last, and meeting bless,
and turn into one truth in singleness.

To Another Housewife

Do you remember how we went,
on duty bound, to feed the crowd
of hungry dogs your father kept
as rabbit-hunters? Lean and loud,
half-starved and furious, how they leapt
against their chains, as though they meant
in mindless rage for being fed,
to tear our childish hands instead!

With tomahawk and knife we hacked
the flyblown tatters of old meat,
gagged at their carcass-smell, and threw
the scraps and watched the hungry eat.
Then turning faint, we made a pact,
(two greensick girls), crossed hearts and swore
to touch no meat forever more.

How many cuts of choice and prime
our housewife hands have dressed since then—
these hands with love and blood imbrued—
for daughters, sons, and hungry men!
How many creatures bred for food
we've raised and fattened for the time
they met at last the steaming knife
that serves the feast of death-in-life!

And as the evening meal is served
we hear the turned-down radio
begin to tell the evening news
just as the family joint is carved.
O murder, famine, pious wars...
Our children shrink to see us so,
in sudden meditation, stand
with knife and fork in either hand.

The Encounter

Lord, how the creatures bully me!
Stroke me, the cat says.
My vibrant velvet lit with eyes
asks you to stroke it.

Look at me, says the horse—
my arches of suave muscle,
my round kind eye, my stride and speed
ask you to fill their need.

And in the rockpools of the shore
creatures like flowers and jewels
wait dumbly for my eyes' translation,
decked for our moment's meeting and no more.

I cannot know my beauty
—say all the creatures—
till you interpret me in god-made words.
Before the falling of your final fire
destroys us all—men, plants and birds—
turn your mad destined eyes this way and see
creation's dew still falling here in me.

Lord, how the earth and the creatures look at me.

Eurydice in Hades

I knew this long ago, when we first loved;
but time went on so well, I had forgotten
what I saw then: how sudden it would be
when the path fell in,
when hand tore out of hand, and I went down
into this region of clay corridors
below the reach of song.

Now I can never hear you, nor you me.
Down these blind passages condemned to wander,
dreams plague me, and my heart
swings like a rocking-horse a child's abandoned.

Singer, creator, come and pierce this clay
with one keen grief, with one redeeming call.
Earth would relent to hear it, if you sang.

As once I dreamed you came.
Some music-maker led me with your voice
upwards; I still remember
one summoning glance of incandescent light
blue as the days I knew.
I saw his laurel-wreath, his mourning mouth:
he had your very look.

And then I dreamed
the King's long shout of triumph, and a voice
that cried "All's lost". And silence fell.
I grope my way through silences like clouds.
And still that phrase of music always murmurs,
but fainter, farther, like your eyes receding.

Your all-creating, all-redeeming song
fades, as the daylight fades.

Elinor Wylie

Born in 1885 in Somerville, New Jersey, Elinor Wylie was a member of the prominent Hoyt family. When her father, Henry Martin Hoyt, became assistant attorney general in 1897, the family moved to Washington, D.C., where Wylie was raised as a socialite. In spite of her desire to continue her education, she was forced by her parents to leave school and lead the life of a debutante.

She married Philip Simmons Hichborn in 1905 and had a son by him in 1907. Three years later she left her husband and child for Horace Wylie, a married lawyer. The couple moved to England in an attempt to avoid the ensuing scandal. Abroad, she anonymously published her first book of poetry, *Incidental Numbers* (1912), which included poems she later refused to contain in her collected works. She and Wylie returned to the United States before World War I and were married in 1916, despite a growing strain in their relationship. In 1920 four of her poems were accepted by *Poetry* magazine; however, the beginning of her literary career marked the end of her second marriage. She left her husband and moved to New York City.

Wylie's next book of poetry, *Nets To Catch the Wind* (1921), was critically acclaimed. It was quickly followed by a substantial amount of work, including the books, *Black Armour* (1923), *Trivial Breath* (1928), and *Angels and Earthly Creatures* (1929). Her first novel, *Jennifer Lorn: A Sedate Extravaganza* (1923) was followed by three more. During 1923 Wylie married the poet William Rose Benét, and though she found this marriage to be a disappointment as well, she did not divorce him. She considered the most intense love relationship of her life to be the one she had with Henry Woodhouse, just before her death from a stroke in Benét's home, December of 1928.

Like her friend, Edna St. Vincent Millay, Wylie wrote poetry in traditional forms, using rhyme, meter, and the sonnet cycle to express her quite modern perceptions. Her best work captures the tension between her belief and disappointment in love, as well as her ambition to excel as a poet and her concept of femininity.

Madman's Song

Better to see your cheek grown hollow,
Better to see your temple worn,
Than to forget to follow, follow,
After the sound of a silver horn.

Better to bind your brow with willow
And follow, follow until you die,
Than to sleep with your head on a golden pillow,
Nor lift it up when the hunt goes by.

Better to see your cheek grown sallow
And your hair grown gray, so soon, so soon,
Than to forget to hallo, hallo,
After the milk-white hounds of the moon.

Atavism

I always was afraid of Somes's Pond:
Not the little pond, by which the willow stands,
Where laughing boys catch alewives in their hands
In brown, bright shallows; but the one beyond.
There, when the frost makes all the birches burn
Yellow as cow-lilies, and the pale sky shines
Like a polished shell between black spruce and pines,
Some strange thing tracks us, turning where we turn.

You'll say I dream it, being the true daughter
Of those who in old times endured this dread.
Look! Where the lily-stems are showing red
A silent paddle moves below the water,
A sliding shape has stirred them like a breath;
Tall plumes surmount a painted mask of death.

A Crowded Trolley Car

The rain's cold grains are silver-gray
Sharp as golden sands,
A bell is clanging, people sway
Hanging by their hands.

Supple hands, or gnarled and stiff,
Snatch and catch and grope;
That face is yellow-pale, as if
The fellow swung from rope.

Dull like pebbles, sharp like knives,

Glances strike and glare,
Fingers tangle, Bluebeard's wives
Dangle by the hair.

Orchard of the strangest fruits
Hanging from the skies;
Brothers, yet insensate brutes
Who fear each other's eyes.

One man stands as free men stand,
As if his soul might be
Brave, unbroken; see his hand
Nailed to an oaken tree.

Winter Sleep

When against earth a wooden heel
Clicks as loud as stone and steel,
When snow turns flour instead of flakes,
And frost bakes clay as fire bakes,
When the hard-bitten fields at last
Crack like iron flawed in the cast,
When the world is wicked and cross and old,
I long to be quit of the cruel cold.

Little birds like bubbles of glass
Fly to other Americas,
Birds as bright as sparkles of wine
Fly in the night to the Argentine,
Birds of azure and flame-birds go
To the tropical Gulf of Mexico:
They chase the sun, they follow the heat,

It is sweet in their bones, O sweet, sweet, sweet!
It's not with them that I'd love to be,
But under the roots of the balsam tree.

Just as the spiniest chestnut-burr
Is lined within with the finest fur,
So the stony-walled, snow-roofed house
Of every squirrel and mole and mouse
Is lined with thistledown, sea-gull's feather,
Velvet mullein-leaf, heaped together
With balsam and juniper, dry and curled,
Sweeter than anything else in the world.
O what a warm and darksome nest
Where the wildest things are hidden to rest!
It's there that I'd love to lie and sleep,
Soft, soft, soft, and deep, deep, deep!

Now That Your Eyes Are Shut

Now that your eyes are shut
Not even a dusty butterfly may brush them;
My flickering knife has cut
Life from sonorous lion throats to hush them.

If pigeons croon too loud
Or lambs bleat proudly, they must come to
    slaughter,
And I command each cloud
To be precise in spilling silent water.

Let light forbear those lids;
I have forbidden the feathery ash to smutch them;

The spider thread that thrids
The gray-plumed grass has not my leave to touch
  them.

My casual ghost may slip,
Issuing tiptoe, from the pure inhuman;
The tissues of my lip
Will bruise your eyelids, while I am a woman.

Innocent Landscape

Here is no peace, although the air has fainted,
  And footfalls die and are buried in deep grass,
And reverential trees are softly painted
  Like saints upon an oriel of glass.

The pattern of the atmosphere is spherical,
  A bubble in the silence of the sun,
Blown thinner by the very breath of miracle
  Around a core of loud confusion.

Here is no virtue; here is nothing blessèd
  Save this foredoomed suspension of the end;
Faith is the blossom, but the fruit is cursèd;
  Go hence, for it is useless to pretend.

INDEX

Poet and translator names are in bold; poem titles are in italics; and poem first lines are in quotations.

ACKNOWLEDGEMENTS

Permission to reprint copyrighted poems is gratefully acknowledged to the following:

ALLEN & UNWIN (PUBLISHERS) LTD., for "Shells," "The Locked Gates," "Kore in Hades," "The Wilderness," "A Bad Dream," and "Told in a Dream" from *Collected Poems* by Kathleen Raine.

MARTIN ALLWOOD, for "Strontium," "The Trees are Naked," "The Women Thought Christ Risen," and "At the Street Corner" by Eeva-Liisa Manner, from *Modern Scandinavian Poetry* ed. and trans. by Martin Allwood.

ANGUS & ROBERTSON (U.K.) LTD., for "Blue Arab," "Woman to Man," "Woman to Child," "For My Daughter," "The Other Half," "To Another Housewife," "The Encounter," and "Eurydice in Hades" from *Collected Poems 1942-1970* by Judith Wright.

BEACON PRESS, for "Roman Poem Number Two," "On Your Love," "West Coast Episode," and "Poem: Of Nightsong and Flight" from *Things That I Do in the Dark: Selected Poems* by June Jordan. Copyright © 1977 by June Jordan.

BLACK SPARROW PRESS, for "George Washington Sends a Pair of Shoebuckles to the Buddha on His Birthday," "The Elephant & the Butterfly Meet on the Buddha's Birthday," and "Sun Gods Have Sun Spots" from *Dancing on the Grave of a Son of a Bitch* by Diane Wakoski. Copyright © 1973 by Diane Wakoski.

BOUNDARY 2, for "Then They Paraded Pompey's Urn," "The Wooden Horse Then Said," and "The Crusaders" by Jenny Mastoraki, from *boundary 2*, Winter 1973.

GWENDOLYN BROOKS, for "A Song in the Front Yard," "The Murder," "Strong Men, Riding Horses," "We Real Cool," "Mrs. Small," "Jessie Mitchell's Mother," "A Sunset of the City," and "To a Winter Squirrel" from *The World of Gwendolyn Brooks*. Copyright © 1971 by Gwendolyn Brooks.

CENTURY HUTCHINSON PUBLISHING GROUP LTD., for "Apology," "The Difference," "Vision of the Cuckoo," and "The Serious Child" from *Collected Poems 1926-66* by Ruth Pitter. Copyright © 1968 by Ruth Pitter.

JOAN DAVES AND JEROME ROTHENBERG, for "Curriculum Vitae" by Ingeborg Bachmann, translated by Jerome Rothenberg. Copyright © 1956, 1957 by R. Piper & Co. Verlag. English translation copyright 1959 by Jerome Rothenberg.

STAVROS DELIGIORGIS, for "Hills Picking Up the Moonlight" by Nina Cassian. English translation copyright © 1980 by Stavros Deligiorgis.

DOUBLEDAY & COMPANY, INC., for "A Valentine for Ben Franklin Who Drives a Truck in California," copyright © 1972, 1975, 1976, 1978 by Diane Wakoski. "The Rings" and "Tearing Up My Mother's Letters," copyright © 1977 by Modern Poetry Association. All poems by Diane Wakoski from the book *The Man Who Shook Hands*. "The Stars" and "Deliverance" by Ping Hsin from *Twentieth Century Chinese Poetry* edited by Kai-yu Hsu. Copyright © 1963 by Kai-yu Hsu. "To a Prize Bird" from *Observations* by Marianne Moore.

EAST AFRICAN PUBLISHING HOUSE LIMITED AND NOÉMIA DE SOUSA, for "If You Want To Know Me" and "The Poem of João" from *When Bullets Begin To Flower*, translated by Margaret Dickinson.

THE ECCO PRESS, for "Descending Figure," "Swans," "The Mirror," and "Lamentations" from *Descending Figure* by Louise Glück. Copyright © 1976, 1977, 1979, 1980 by Louise Glück. Published by The Ecco Press in 1980.

ESTATE OF NORMA MILLAY ELLIS, for "Spring," "The Bean-Stalk," "English Sparrows," and "The Rabbit" from *Collected Poems* (Harper & Row) by Edna St. Vincent Millay. Copyright © 1921, 1939, 1948, 1967 by Edna St. Vincent Millay and Norma Millay Ellis.

ESTATE OF INGRID JONKER, for "Dark Stream" from *Selected Poems* (Jonathan Cape Ltd.) by Ingrid Jonker. Translated from the Afrikaans by Jack Cope and William Plomer.

FARRAR, STRAUS & GIROUX, INC., for "O the Chimneys,"

Jr., Executor of the Estate of Anne Sexton. "Pain for a Daughter" from *Live or Die* by Anne Sexton. Copyright © 1966 by Anne Sexton.

HOUSE OF ANANSI PRESS LIMITED, for "The City Planners" from *The Circle Game* by Margaret Atwood (Toronto: House of Anansi Press). Copyright © 1966 by Margaret Atwood.

OLWYN HUGHES, for "Where Does This Tenderness Come From?," "Poems for Akhmatova," and "Readers of Newspapers" from *Selected Poems of Marina Tsvetayeva*, published by Hutchinsons, London. Translation copyright © 1971, 1986 by Elaine Feinstein.

INDIANA UNIVERSITY PRESS, for "The Roosters Will Crow" by Cecília Meireles, from *Modern Brazilian Poetry: An Anthology*, translated and edited by John Nist with Yolanda Leite. Copyright © 1962 by Indiana University Press. "Time Caught in a Net," "Tirzah and the Wide World," "How Hong Kong Was Destroyed," "A Private View," and "Poem of Explanation" by Dahlia Ravikovitch, from *Israeli Poetry*, selected and translated by Warren Bargad and Stanley Chyet. Copyright © 1986 by Indiana University Press.

INTERNATIONAL CREATIVE MANAGEMENT, INC., for "Absalom" from *U.S. 1* by Muriel Rukeyser. Copyright © 1938 and 1962 by Muriel Rukeyser. "A Game of Ball" and "Then I Saw What the Calling Was" from *Beast in View* by Muriel Rukeyser. Copyright © 1944 and 1968 by Muriel Rukeyser. "St. Roach" from *The Gates* by Muriel Rukeyser. Copyright © 1976 by Muriel Rukeyser.

ALFRED A. KNOPF, INC., for "Medallion," copyright © 1962 by Sylvia Plath. "Spinster," copyright © 1961 by Sylvia Plath. Reprinted from *The Colossus and Other Poems* by Sylvia Plath. "The Window of the Woman Burning" from *The Twelve-Spoked Wheel Flashing* by Marge Piercy. Copyright © 1978 by Marge Piercy. "The Deck That Pouts," "The World Comes Back Like an Old Cat," "Mornings in Various Years," and "Ascending Scale" from *Stone, Paper, Knife* by Marge Piercy. Copyright © 1983 by Marge Piercy. "Madman's Song," "Atavism," "A Crowded Trolley Car," "Now That Your Eyes Are Shut," "Innocent Landscape," and

Hell," "Away, Melancholy," "Fafnir and the Knights," "Harold's Leap," "The Wanderer," "Love Me!," and "Now Pine-Needles" from *Collected Poems* by Stevie Smith. Copyright © 1972 by Stevie Smith. "Sea Rose," "The Wind Sleepers," "Cities," "The Walls Do Not Fall" (sections 6, 13, 14), and "The Flowering of the Rod" (sections 6, 7, 9, 10) from *Collected Poems* by H.D. Copyright © 1982 by the Estate of Hilda Doolittle. "I Fire at the Face of the Country Where I Was Born" and "A Chinese Ulysses" by Kazuko Shiraishi and "Mother" by Nagase Kiyoko from *Women Poets of Japan*. Copyright © 1977 by Kenneth Rexroth and Ikuko Atsumi. "Remembering," "For the Record," and selections from "Multitudinous Stars and Spring Waters" from *Women Poets of China*. Copyright © 1972 by Kenneth Rexroth and Ling Chung.

NEW RIVERS PRESS for "Into the Silence of the Forest," "Assimilation," and "From My Life I Make a Poem" by Eeva-Liisa Manner, translated by Aili Jarvenpa. Translation copyright © by New Rivers Press and Aili Jarvenpa.

PETER OWEN LTD., LONDON, for "A Man" and "Self-Portrait" by Nina Cassian, from *Anthology of Contemporary Romanian Poetry* ed. and trans. by Roy MacGregor-Hastie.

PERSEA BOOKS, INC., for "Fog Land" and "Exile" by Ingeborg Bachmann from *German Poetry 1910-1975*, edited and translated by Michael Hamburger. Translation copyright © 1976, 1977 by Michael Hamburger.

RANDOM HOUSE, INC., for "Tender Buttons," "A Frightful Release," "A Purse," "A Mounted Umbrella," "Eye Glasses," "A Cutlet," "Water Raining," "A Sound," "A Table," "Suppose an Eyes," and "Rhubarb" from *Selected Writings of Gertrude Stein*. Copyright © 1946 by Random House, Inc.

SIMON & SCHUSTER, INC., for "They Eat Out" and "Owl Song" from *Selected Poems* by Margaret Atwood. Copyright © 1976 by Margaret Atwood.

ST. MARTIN'S PRESS, INC., for "& Then," "Senses of Heritage," "Inquiry," and "Resurrection of the Daughter" from *Nappy Edges* by Ntozake Shange. Copyright © 1972, 1974, 1975, 1976, 1977, 1978 by Ntozake Shange.

FADWA TUQUAN, for "After Twenty Years" and "From